The Work of the Church Officer

Glenn H. Asquith

JUDSON PRESS
PUBLISHERS SINCE 1824
VALLEY FORGE, PA

The Work of the Church Officer
© 2009 by Judson Press, Valley Forge, PA 19482-0851
Originally published as Church Officers of Work (revised edition)
Copyright © 1977 by Judson Press, Valley Forge, PA 19482-0851
All rights reserved.

Unless otherwise indicated, Bible quotations in this volume are
in accordance with the Revised Standard Version of the Bible,
copyright © 1946, 1952, 1971, by the Division of Christian
Education of the National Council of the Churches of Christ in the
U.S.A. Used by permission.

Library of Congress Cataloging-in-Publication Data

Asquith, Glenn H.
   The work of the church officer / Glenn H. Asquith. -- 1st, rev. ed.
      p. cm.
   Previously published as: Church officers at work. 1977.
   Includes index.
   ISBN 978-0-8170-1639-5 (pbk. : alk. paper) 1. Baptists--
Government. 2. Church officers--Baptists. I. Asquith, Glenn H.
Church officers at work. II. Title.
   BX6346.A87 2009
   262'.06--dc22

                                   2009042389

Printed in the U.S.A.

First Edition, 2009.

Concerning the Author

The Reverend Glenn H. Asquith, D.D., received his formal education in the public schools of Rochester, New York, at what is now Eastern College (B.A.), and at Eastern Baptist Theological Seminary (Th.B.). Additional work was taken at Temple University and in continuing education programs. In 1952 his seminary awarded him the Doctor of Divinity degree. In 1975 he was selected as one of seven to receive Fiftieth Anniversary Alumni Awards by the seminary.

He has had six notable pastorates: First Baptist Church, Manayunk, Philadelphia, Pennsylvania; First Baptist Church, Salem, New Jersey; First Baptist Church (now part of Central Baptist Church), Westerly, Rhode Island; Asylum Avenue Baptist Church, Hartford, Connecticut; First United Baptist Church, Lowell, Massachusetts; First Baptist Church, Montclair, New Jersey.

From 1950 to 1956 he was Executive Secretary of the New York State Baptist Convention. During that period he served on many denominational boards and committees and on Governor Harriman's Advisory Committee for a Conference on the Aging.

He spent 1960 and 1961 as Executive Secretary of the Philadelphia Baptist Association. While in that position he was invited to be part of the White House Conference on the Aging.

From 1961 to 1967 he was the Executive Director of the Division of Christian Publications of the American Baptist Board of Education and Publication, and had a large part in developing the curriculum resources known as the Christian Faith and Work Plan.

He is the author of many articles, tracts, poems, etc., and of twelve books: *A Two-Century Church*, *Church Officers at Work*, *Lively May I Walk*, *Selected Works of Ryters Krampe*, *Cousin Tom*, *Preaching According to Plan*, *The Person I Am*, *Death Is All Right*, *God in My Day*, *Living in the Presence of God*, *Footprints in the Sand*, and *Living Creatively as an Older Adult*.

Since retirement he has served several churches as interim pastor.

This wide experience has qualified him eminently to produce helpful materials for church officials.

Contents

Preface

This little book has had a long history, but after twenty-five years and sixteen printings its purpose is the same: "To answer the questions raised by pastors and committees relative to the particular responsibility for the church life and program to be carried by each elected or appointed official."

Commissioned first as a text for a leadership course in administration, *Church Officers at Work* met with such wide approval that it was offered as a trade book. Missionaries and denominational field workers, as well as pastors, have testified to the usefulness of the book. Newly organized churches and well-established churches have found guidance and suggestions for the efficient operation of a local congregation.

This new revision of the original text includes special help for a church nominating committee. Of all church committees, it would be difficult to find another that bears such a heavy and strategic task in the life of a church.

The author has faith that the future contribution of this book will be as great as, or greater than, the record of the past.

Glenn H. Asquith
June, 1976

"And his gifts were that some should be apostles, some prophets, some evangelists, some pastors and teachers, to equip the saints for the work of ministry, for building up the body of Christ."

—Ephesians 4:11-12

Chapter 1

A Church Working Democratically

Why We Need Church Officers

If we go back no further than Pentecost to locate the first New Testament church, the group that gathered following the inspired preaching of Peter and his companions on that wondrous day in Jerusalem described in Acts 2, we shall find that there were no church officers—unless the preacher of the day might be called an officer—and no duties. Where there is nothing to be done, workers are not needed. That first church had no roll of members as yet, with names and street addresses to be kept up-to-date, no bank account to be kept balanced, no bills to be paid, no buildings to be maintained. But as the months and years went on, of course, that church found one problem of administration after another, and each had to be solved. One by one, church offices were created to meet needs as they arose. This, also, is the basis accepted by churches today: the need coupled with the simplest and most efficient way of caring for it.

Polity and Practice

"Polity" is a word rarely used by the average person of today, but it persists in church documents. It is derived from a Greek word meaning "government," and it has come to mean the form of government of a church. We can think of the polity of the church, our church, as the recognized principles underlying the day-by-day working of the church. It is the unwritten constitution and bylaws against which all action is tested. There are two general types of church polity to be found among denominations and churches today—episcopal and congregational. There are shades and variations of each, but, for the most part, a church will subscribe in a general way to one or the other of these. The episcopal type is fairly authoritarian, with final decisions vested in a bishop or a hierarchy of over-bishops. Congregational polity is democratic in the sense that final decisions are vested in the membership of the church. (Presbyterianism is a form of congregational polity.) Congregational polity, which Baptist (and some other denominations) hold as their New Testament birthright, will be discussed here.

To understand Baptist church polity, it will be necessary to go back to the beginnings. The primary tenet of Baptist churches is that the New Testament is the sufficient and only acceptable rule of faith and order. Whatever is found in the New Testament in reference to church government, then, will be received in preference to other historical precedent, expediency, or ecclesiastical tradition. And this is found: any group of believers coming together regularly for worship and service may be honored as being a "church." As did the early apostles, members defer to the decisions of the gathered church in the matters of setting apart men and women for the work of ministry, in the choice of deacons, and in the taking of voluntary offerings for the needy in the parish or in far places. This power of the church we speak of as "autonomy," the right of self-government.

Autonomy works out with great similarity in churches despite the freedom involved. Starting from the same principle, most churches come out at the same destination of self-imposed rules and self-set standards of achievement, although the routes taken may not correspond exactly.

The Church Pattern Produced by Democratic Autonomy

Democracy in a church or nation does not imply haphazardness or a denial of all authority. The systematic procedures, however, are instituted and maintained by democratic action, and the authority is self-imposed. The voting membership in a Baptist church is, and must be always, the body of final reference and the holder of the veto power. Voting membership is the term used in order to distinguish between regular membership and limited membership (in some churches called "associate membership") made up of those who have not, for one reason or another, fulfilled all requirements for full membership—such as students away from the home church, "watch-care" members temporarily absent from home churches, the nonimmersed in churches recognizing only this form of baptism, and so forth. In some churches these affiliated, or associate, members have the right of voting on some matters and not on others.

To help in the understanding of how a self-governing church operates, it may help to think of three separate functions, such as those exercised by our federal government:

EXECUTIVE	LEGISLATIVE	JUDICIAL
The Staff:	The Church	Advisory Council
Pastor and other staff	Voting Membership	General Committee, or Executive Board

1. *Legislative*

The voting membership, the legislative branch of the church government, meets in accordance with the provisions of the constitution adopted at the time of the organization of the church and since revised (probably many, many times!). An annual meeting is held in most Baptist churches, and semiannual, quarterly, and monthly meetings are the rule in some churches. In addition to these regular meetings, all churches make provisions for special and emergency meetings. It is a rare church that can nurture its democratic character and go through a full year from annual meeting to annual meeting without the necessity for special meetings to decide some urgent questions. The privileges and responsibilities of the voting membership are many.

(*a*) The regulation of the voting membership itself is no small job. The constitution provides for admission and exclusion of members, and the church is bound by these provisions until it abrogates or amends them. When there is an applicant for admission to the membership, a person who has made a satisfactory declaration of faith and is eligible to enter the church fellowship by one of the approved methods, the usual procedure is for the pastor to recommend him or her to the board of deacons. After the deacons are satisfied concerning the sincerity and qualifications of the applicant, they will recommend that one be received into the membership. The voting membership will then take whatever action it deems best. In matter of dismission—requests for letters of transfer, resignations, erasure of names of long inactive members, a clearing of the rolls of those who cannot be located, and so forth—the same general procedure will be followed. This part of church business is important because the membership roll is the basis of all church activity and progress. The quality and amount of work done, the standing of a church in its community, and its future mission depend upon the members who make up the church. Carelessness in this part of the responsibility quite often results in a growing list of inactive and nonresident members.

(b) Second in importance to the control of the membership is the determining of the financial policy of the church. Very little can be done by elected or appointed officials without an appropriation of money. The power of a budget carefully drawn up, carefully balanced, and carefully adopted cannot be overestimated. When a member votes for a proposed budget, he or she is expressing views on hundreds of issues that are automatically disposed of by the various appropriations. It is important that the items be carefully examined and that the implications of the budget be understood by the membership since so much depends on its approval or rejection.

(c) Calling a pastor is another important duty of the voting membership. In this discussion it is subordinated to the membership and financial actions only because it is an infrequent item of business. However, when the need arises, the voting membership must declare for or against the candidate. Of course, much of the responsibility for finding a pastor will be upon the pulpit committee (to be dealt with in chapter 2).

(*d*) The voting membership has another time-consuming task. The reports of boards and committees will come up for approval and ratification at the end of the church year. Important trends in church activity and thought are reflected in the annual reports of the various chairpersons and other officials. The reports need to be checked against the authority that was granted at the time the boards or committees were created and the officials elected. Progress should be noted with thanksgiving.

Beyond these privileges and powers of the voting membership, most of the work is parceled out among committees and elected officials. Later chapters will deal with this part of the church program.

Thus, the legislative branch of the local church government, the voting membership, charts the course for the church, elects officials, appoints committees, allocates the money, and holds the power of veto or censure for unauthorized actions of members or boards.

2. *Executive*

(*a*) The pastor, in some churches referred to as the minister, heads up the staff, which represents the executive branch of the church. The pastor is responsible to the church as a whole for the conduct of his or her work, although some churches may have a pastoral relations committee to review the work, make suggestions, and offer constructive criticism. But, even with such a committee, a pastor in a regular or specially called meeting may appeal to the church if he or she considers that any decisions of the committee are unwise or unfair.

A capable pastor who has been in a church long enough to gain the respect and confidence of the people is apt to be in the dangerous position of accepted dictator. Like George Washington, a pastor may repeatedly refuse the crown without changing the fact in the hearts of many of the people. The average member of a church has little skill or knowledge especially related to the conduct of a religious institution. The member recognizes this fact and, at the same time, knows that the pastor has spent many years in preparation, has profited by years of experience, and is thus qualified to be the leader. The member may think herself to be like a minor stockholder in a telephone company at a meeting of the corporation—the stockholder has no skill in repairing or installing telephones or planning the services to a large community; so why should such a one use one's voting power to control the management that is so ably caring for the business? Why, thinks a church member, should I go against the best judgment of my highly skilled pastor? As a consequence there is the temptation for a member to be inclined to "give the pastor what he wants." The pastor needs to be constantly aware of this and to insist on hearing the opinions of the members.

(1) The pastor, then, usually initiates legislation. Beyond the routine business of church meetings, much of the discussion and action will be on matters suggested by the pastor. The church maintains its democratic character by restricting

the pastor's power to specifically pastoral functions and by requiring that anything outside that field be submitted to the church. Even though the action may be in accordance with the best judgment of the pastor, nevertheless it is the church that makes the suggestion an act. Democratic procedures are slow, but they are likely to be sure and satisfactory in the end. The executive branch of our national government recognizes this fact, and so must the executive branch of a church.

(2) The larger share of the pastor's work is likely to be on the other side of the ledger. The pastor will initiate much legislation, to be sure, but his or her principal task will be to carry out the purpose of the church as expressed in the constitution and bylaws, in the amendments, and in actions taken year by year. This work is summed up in the constitution of one church in these words: "The pastor shall preach, attend meetings of the advisory board, and in general perform the duties common to pastors in evangelical churches." This is not very definite but is about as detailed as a similar clause in the average church constitution. The "duties common to pastors in evangelical churches" are all-inclusive. The pastor will be expected to preach, teach, call, perform marriage ceremonies, conduct funeral services, represent the church at denominational meetings, and be available to relevant community projects. The pastor has the responsibility for organizing the work of the church, including the church school, and for keeping the overall organization running smoothly. His or her advice will be sought by the committees of the church and by its elected officials. He or she will be the promoter of specific projects voted at church meetings. And, if there is a

staff, the pastor will be required to keep all positions filled and direct the work of the persons involved.

(3) Not many churches will require a complete staff, and many will have no one but the pastor. Other churches may have a staff including an assistant pastor or a pastor's assistant, a director of Christian education, one church secretary or several, a director of music, and at least one custodian. In the discussion that follows, each of these positions will be treated separately, while recognizing that in some churches two or more of the functions may be combined and carried out by one person. The pastor will direct the staff by individual conferences and by general staff meetings.

(*b*) The assistant pastor may be an ordained man or woman, or a student from a theological seminary or other training school. He or she may be a young person gaining experience for a church to be served later, or an older person who has relinquished the heavier duties of a full-time pastorate. It is customary for the pastor to locate a person for this position and then submit the name to the pulpit committee, advisory board, or other group bearing the responsibility for the oversight of this part of the work. Occasionally, church action is required. An assistant pastor is responsible directly to the pastor and his or her duties will be outlined by the pastor.

(*c*) The pastor's assistant may be a retired minister or a lay person with training or natural inclination for the work. The title "church visitor" is used sometimes instead of pastor's assistant. Like the assistant pastor, this person is selected by the pastor and is responsible to the pastor. The chief task will be that of parish calling. This assistant will follow up leads to prospective members and refer these to the pastor. Calls on the families of the church will enable the assistant to keep the pastor in touch with the needs of the members.

(*d*) The director of Christian education occupies a strategic position in a church and is engaged, usually, by the board of Christian education working with the pastor and advisory board. Many churches require a church vote on the call of this person. The director works closely with the pastor and must keep the program in harmony with that of the pastor. The board of Christian education will meet with the director regularly and, sometimes, the board of deacons will undertake to review the work and make suggestions. With the approval of the pastor and the board of Christian education, the director may initiate legislation relevant to the task at hand.

The prime responsibility of the director will be the church school; the second task in importance will be the coordination of all phases of Christian education in the church. Girl Scouts, Boy Scouts, vacation church school, children's activities, and special programs for special days (such as Children's Day) will be parts of a total program. A long-range program may be planned in consultation with the pastor and board. The director's tenure of office does not necessarily coincide with that of the pastor, although the director must be advised to work in harmony with a new pastor—otherwise a resignation is in order.

(*e*) The church secretary may be engaged by the pastor or by the personnel committee of the church in consultation with the pastor. This person will be responsible mainly to the pastor. The qualifications for this job will go beyond a simple ability with the typewriter and dictating machine, for there will be calls to act as a buffer between the members of the church (and outsiders) and the staff. The work will include things to be done for many groups and organizations and may entail the planning of the church bulletins and newsletters. Many decisions will devolve on the secretary. Tact is a distinct asset of this position.

(f) A director of music may or may not be the organist or pianist. Where there are two people sharing the responsibility, the organist or pianist may or may not be counted as a member of the staff. This work will be discussed fully under the Music Committee.

(g) The custodian (called by other names: building engineer, sexton, janitor, maintenance man or woman) is engaged by and is responsible to the board of trustees or building committee in consultation with the pastor. The job is that of keeping the building clean and in good order, making repairs that call for minor adjustments, reporting the need for major repairs, keeping the lawns and greenery trimmed. The custodian will be required to keep aware of all meetings to be held in the building and to see that rooms are warm or cool and ventilated according to the season, have the doors unlocked at the right times, and to lock up after all activities of the day have been concluded. In a large church, the custodian may have assistants to do the manual labor while giving direction as supervisor. The custodian may have the task of changing the letters on the outside bulletin boards. Tables must be set up for dinners, the church prepared for weddings and funerals and straightened up afterward. After a service of worship, the pews should be inspected and discarded bulletins, and so forth, be removed; pencils and registration cards must be kept in the pew racks. The public will judge a church somewhat by the result of the efficiency of the custodian.

In a small church without a custodian, the pastor should never be expected to take over this work; volunteers from the congregation should take turns in doing what is required.

3. *Judicial*

In addition to the legislative group (voting membership) and the executive branch (pastor and staff), there is the judicial branch of the church government (advisory board or general committee, advisory committee, executive committee).

(*a*) The advisory board (or equivalent group) varies as to membership, but usually a body of this kind is made up of all the elected officials of the church plus the presidents of the societies— such as men's fellowship or club, women's society, and youth fellowship. In addition, some churches elect from three to five members-at-large at the annual meeting. The aim is to secure a complete representation of all activities within the church program. If this endeavor is successful, there will be no organized group within the church unaware of the plans and programs of the entire church. The board will hold regular monthly meetings, with the possible exception of the two summer months (July-August).

The board is an organized group, with a chairperson and secretary selected at the first meeting following the annual meeting of the church. Some churches prefer that the pastor serve as permanent chairperson, but this has the disadvantage of putting the pastor in the middle of arguments. Also, the chairperson is limited in the expression of opinion and if the pastor sits as a member, he or she has the privilege of speaking to any points.

The order of business at a regular meeting of the advisory board will include the following items, with local variations. The chairperson will call the meeting to order. A devotional period may follow. The minutes will be read and approved. The church treasurer's report of the month's financial transactions, and the benevolence (or financial) treasurer's report of the month's receipts and disbursements will be received. The building committee will report on the condition of the building. Other necessary reports will be made, and then any old business will be picked up from the minutes to be disposed of or referred for later action. New business will occupy the remaining time.

(b) The nature of the business justifies the term "judicial branch." Any matter that an individual or organization proposes to bring before a church meeting should be cleared by the advisory board. This board is so representative that it protects the democratic right of all members, and it is small enough to be efficient. A suggested item of business will be discussed with the view of determining whether or not it requires church action; it is possible that the board itself, or some other organization of the church, has jurisdiction and can act upon the matter. The items that are considered important enough to require church action will be referred to the clerk of the church for placing on the agenda of the next church meeting. If there is urgency, the advisory board will ask for a special meeting of the church. In the meantime, a subcommittee will be appointed by the board to gather the facts on the business to be presented. This will save time and permit intelligent action.

(c) From the other direction, items of business passed by the church may need interpretation. There may be an uncertainty, for instance, as to the jurisdiction of the deacons or the board of Christian education concerning some item that seems to involve both. The advisory board will decide this and authorize the proper organization to carry out the church's instructions.

Many times the pastor will wish to consult with the advisory board before doing something out of the ordinary and beyond what is usually expected. The church may have suggested that a particular sermon of the pastor be printed and distributed. Before requisitioning money for this project, the pastor will be well advised to have the recommendation of the advisory board. By referring doubtful issues to the board, the pastor will protect himself or herself from criticism and maintain a spirit of harmony. In churches that have an advisory board (or its equivalent), the constitution will define the field of authority and usually give the board power to act on all ordinary matters of business in the interim between regular church meetings.

Communication

The breakdown of communication between and among the officers of a church accounts for many of the problems that beset an average church. The right hand must always know what the left hand is doing, and vice versa. In church affairs there is no room for secretiveness, no place for one organization or individual to try for a "scoop" by doing something before others are aware of what is happening. In one church a deacon caught rumors that the people were dissatisfied with the hymnals; he assumed that they were complaining because the bindings were worn and quietly sent the books out (between Sundays) and had them rebound at his own expense. The truth was that there was a desire for a more up-to-date book. In more important matters than this, independent working can cause serious harm and division. If a church has no advisory board (or equivalent), there should be some method devised to bring all the officers and chairpersons together at least once a month for complete and frank reports.

Helpful Books for Further Investigation

Goodwin, Everett C., *The New Hiscox Guide for Baptist Churches*. Valley Forge: Judson Press, 1995.

Grenz, Stanley J., *The Baptist Congregation*. Valley Forge: Judson Press, 1985.

Maring, Norman H., and Hudson, Winthrop S., *A Baptist Manual of Polity and Practice, Revised Edition*. Valley Forge: Judson Press, 1963, 1991.

Vedder, Henry C., *A Short History of the Baptists*. Valley Forge: Judson Press, 1967.

Chapter 2

Yes, Committees Are Necessary!

The Names and Work of Committees

In a church, no matter how small in membership, there are some tasks that cannot be done effectively in open meetings of the entire membership. Information must be secured, data assembled, and spadework done before the matter in hand can be brought forward for intelligent action. Also, there are items of business that recur throughout the year, and projects to be completed that call for special knowledge or ability. The efficient way to take care of these particular tasks is by committee work. A committee may consist of one or more members. The popular size of a committee is three or five. Large assignments may call for larger committees, and "big" churches may wish to have a wider representation on a committee.

Committees are subsidiary to the larger body that created them. In a church there will be committees and subcommittees in every department of the work, but for the present we

17

will look at the major committees of a church. These are appointed or elected in various ways. Nominations for membership on the more important of the committees are brought before the annual meeting of the church, and the persons are selected by ballot just as are the officers. Other committees may be described in the constitution with the provision that the members be appointed by the advisory board or other responsible organization. Yet other committees are appointed by the moderator or chairperson of the church, with or without the ratification of the membership.

After election or appointment, the members of a committee meet to organize. Usually the body creating the committee names one of the members to serve as chairperson, or proceeds on the assumption that the first person named is to be chairperson. Sometimes the person whose name is first on the list is considered to be convener to call the first meeting of the committee, at which time a permanent chairperson is elected. It is customary to elect a secretary at the first meeting. Committees are obligated to report to the parent body according to their instructions. Some committees serve for a year, others until a specific task is completed, others until dismissed by the creating body. And with this general introduction we are ready to look more closely at some of the major church committees.

The Nominating Committee

Probably the most important and influential of all committees is the nominating committee. Despite the fact that church elections are democratic, the election usually confirms the choice of the nominating committee. Thus, the nominating committee practically selects the officers for the coming year. And the officers will lead the church to success or failure; thus, the wisest and best informed from among the church membership need to be utilized on this committee.

Due to the decisive character of its work, the nominating committee should be made up of not fewer than five members. If the church is large, a larger committee is indicated. Inasmuch as the committee affects directly the work of the church, it is elected by the church at the annual meeting and serves until the next annual meeting. In brief, the work of this committee is to present to the church at the annual meeting a complete slate of officers, committee members, and others to fill the vacancies occurring at the end of the current church year.

Elected at the annual meeting, and with a chairperson designated, the nominating committee is ready to go to work. At the first meeting, of course, a secretary will be named, and the members will be cautioned to keep the work of the committee confidential. Working confidentially and quietly, the committee will seek to do its work according to the powers granted to it. The first step will be to make a complete list of the offices to be filled. Not all of the officials of a church will go out of office after a one-year term. The list should include only the offices to be filled.

Taking the offices in turn, the committee will consider first the incumbent, the one now holding the office. Churches have both written and unwritten rules and traditions regarding certain offices. Some offices are considered to be one-year tasks; others, such as the posts of clerk and treasurer, may be thought of as somewhat permanent. For the positions where there is no legal or traditional block against reelection, and where the official is giving good service and is willing to continue in office, the committee usually presents the name of that incumbent. If the committee feels there is a valid reason for a change, sometimes to shift an official to a more important spot, the officer should be consulted. To omit the name of a faithful and willing servant without notification and explanation could be most unwise and disruptive.

For offices where reelection is not customary, the committee will consider the next in line. It is not necessarily true that that person is the best available for the higher office, but there is that possibility. Experience and training have been gained, and there may be expectation of the promotion.

After looking at the incumbent and the next person in line, the committee may have a reservoir of names of officials who have been out of office long enough to be eligible for election. For example: in some churches a person may serve as deacon for three years and then be ineligible for reelection until one year has elapsed since holding the office. The same provisions may be true of other offices, and the committee will do well to consider the people who have been in legal "exile."

After giving due thought to the incumbents, the ones next in line (such as vice-chairpersons, vice-presidents, and so on), and the "exiles," the committee has a free opportunity to discover new names. A complete list of the members of the church should be available for each member of the committee. Insofar as possible, the committee should try to assign the offices proportionately among members of long standing, newer members, men, women, and young people. If a church is fortunate enough to include in the membership people of two or more races, this should be taken into account. Even though one race (white or black, for instance) may be in the majority, the minority group deserves representation on the governing boards of the church. The committee should do its best to break down the old suspicion that "the same people run things all the time" by utilizing heretofore unused and talented people.

When the committee has agreed upon a name for an office, some member of the committee should be appointed to speak to the candidate, outlining simply and definitely the work of the office and asking for permission to include the person's name on the nominating committee's report. It should be explained also that the nomination is no guarantee of election. Until permission is unequivocally given, a name ought not to be included.

When the committee's report is complete, agreement should be reached as to the presentation—usually the chairperson or secretary will read the report when the moderator calls for it at the annual meeting. After the reading, the report should be handed to the clerk of the church.

If the nominating committee is elected annually, it is competent to care for any vacancies that may occur during the year. Unless the constitution reads otherwise, nominations for vacancies or for newly created offices will be presented by the committee at the first regular or special meeting after the need for the nomination occurs.

Unless there is a bylaw forbidding such action, the committee may bring in the name of one of its members for an office. In an efficient church, false modesty is a detriment to the work.

The Music Committee

The church and the nominating committee will do well to remember, when selecting the music committee, that the prime requisites for a useful member of the committee are a knowledge of music, an appreciation of worship values, tact, and, if possible, no family ties with the director of music, organist, or choir members. This is one of the committees elected at the annual meeting and usually for a one-year term. It should not be larger than five members, and three may well suffice.

The responsibility of the music committee concerns the entire music program of the church. It should cooperate, invariably, with the minister in the planning of this program. Ordinarily, this committee is qualified to serve during the year without referring to the church just so long as it keeps within the budgetary allotment for music. In some churches the engaging of a director of music or organist requires the ratification of the church. The director of music, the organist, and any paid choir members or other salaried musicians employed by the church are directly or indirectly responsible to the music committee.

While many music committees serve out their one-year term without facing the necessity of finding a new director of music, the committee is responsible for the quality of the present director's work. If the committee considers the work unsatisfactory, some arrangement for improvement must be made. The director may respond positively to suggestions or criticisms, or the committee may need to replace the person. If for any reason whatever the committee is faced with the necessity of finding a new director, there are certain routine steps to be taken. First, the names of available directors must be obtained; this may be done by reference to schools of music, by discreet advertisements in church papers or newspapers, by conferring with pastors in the community, or by submitting the need to the area or national denominational offices.

After the names of directors have been secured, the committee will go over the list and select two or three whose qualifications seem adequate. If the director is already employed, the committee members may decide to go to the church being served and observe at first hand. When they agree on a good prospect, the committee will make an appointment for the person to visit in the home church where the facilities may be assessed and the need may be outlined. An agreement may be reached at this meeting, or the process may have to be repeated with some other director.

In the event that the music committee is in a church where the director of music is not the organist, the committee may, at some time, be faced with the selection of an organist or pianist. The procedure will be much like that of choosing a director except that the director on the staff may well have a name to present. Ordinarily, an organist must not be engaged without the approval of the director. Also, a prospective organist must have an opportunity to display competence on the organ which will be played Sunday after Sunday. Sometimes it is wise that the prospect try out at a regular church service.

Where there are paid soloists, the music committee may have to fill vacancies from time to time. Here again, names of possibilities may be obtained from the director or organist or both. The committee may wish to set apart an evening convenient to the members for the purpose of listening to soloists. The musicians should not be placed in open rivalry; the auditions should be confidential and as private as possible. Even though the committee has the power of choice, it is unwise to bring in to the program a soloist unacceptable to the director.

The committee is likely to find that professional musicians are easier to deal with than amateurs or volunteers. Inasmuch as many churches have a volunteer choir exclusively, the average music committee must know its responsibilities and duties in this sensitive field. Where there is a volunteer choir, the committee should see to it that the director is a person with ability to teach as well as to plan and conduct. It is a rare church that can muster enough able musicians from within its membership to make teaching unnecessary. If a volunteer choir is thrown open to anyone who is willing to sing, the committee may find itself in a hopeless situation that will take years to solve. The director should be instructed to have a frank conversation with a would-be choir member; perhaps a private tryout could be arranged on a friendly basis. The choir should not be opened to someone who is utterly incapable of singing acceptably, no matter who the applicant may be. Prospects without solid knowledge of choir music might be encouraged to attend choir practice on a spectator or auditor basis with occasional participation. Advancement to substitute might come as progress is noted.

In the long run, the music committee will find that the best way to deal with a volunteer choir is by the establishment of hard-and-fast rules worked out in cooperation with the director. (In a church that cannot afford a director, the volunteer leader will need the strong support of the music committee in the efforts to screen the singers.) For instance, the director may wish to set a requirement that no one may sing on Sunday morning (or whenever the regular service is held) who has not appeared for the weekly rehearsal or practice. This is a reasonable provision which the committee will do well to endorse. Other rules might be: no solos until the director considers the singer qualified, no changing of places in the choir seats—each member will sit where the director feels that that person's voice is needed; substitutes will be used only when the regulars are absent. If a choir is built around rules formulated by the leader, or director, and the music committee, each new singer will understand the situation from the beginning. The committee should bear in mind that the music included in a worship service can strengthen or spoil it.

Other duties of the music committee will include the obtaining of a reasonable appropriation for new music, the fostering of annual music programs, such as at Easter and Christmas, and the providing of an annual recognition of the choir.

The music committee will be required to make a report at the annual meeting following its election.

The Ushers' Committee

The chairperson of ushers is usually an elected officer. He or she is given the privilege of making up the committee, in many churches. In a few churches, the deacons usher in addition to fulfilling their other duties. When this is the rule, often the deacons take turns at being head usher at the morning service, choosing helpers from the general membership. Inasmuch as ushering is an important task in itself, a church usually finds that a special committee is required. But, however the committee is formed, the tasks are the same.

If the chairperson of ushers finds that he or she has enough help, including both older and younger people, to do the job adequately, he or she will first make up a chart of dates and names. A copy of this chart should be provided for each usher. On the chart should be the request that an usher who is unable to keep an appointment as indicated notify the chairperson as far in advance as he or she possibly can.

The main task of the ushers is to greet and seat the congregation at the regular services and at other times when large gatherings are held in the church. The chairperson should not usher people personally except in emergencies; the task is organization, oversight, and greeting. A full half hour before the set time for a service, the chairperson should be in the lobby or narthex of the church prepared to greet the first arrivals. The chairperson's task should not include the distribution of the programs; more important is the giving of a favorable impression of the church to each attendant. The pastor may preach well but fail to bring back a casual attendant who has received a negative impression of the church from the kind of greeting or lack of greeting received at the door. Cheerfulness without familiarity, courtesy without officiousness, friendliness without curiosity mark the good head usher. If a coat rack is provided, the head usher may call this to the attention of anyone unfamiliar with the situation. A spot well within the lobby makes it possible for the head usher to save his or her greeting until the one coming in the door has taken bearings and, possibly, removed a coat. The ushers will respect the accepted intervals for seating latecomers—sometimes denoted by a star on the program or calendar. During prayers and the reading of the Scripture a tactful restraint of anyone attempting to enter the sanctuary is in order.

The position of the assistant ushers will depend upon the architecture of the church building. If there is but one main entrance, there should be two ushers stationed there awaiting the nod of the head usher as people are greeted and passed. Within the church there should be someone at the head of each aisle. After first greeting a person, the head usher will direct the person to an assistant usher who, in turn, will pass the person on to an aisle usher. (A small church will adapt these procedures as required for the space to be covered.) A smooth job of ushering at the peak period of persons entering will do away with an awkward gathering of people at the back of the church, and it will eliminate the wanderers who elect to find seats for themselves. (At this point it may be noted that there are some who sit in the same spot at each service. A wise usher will learn the ways of the members and give all the courtesy of ushering, even though the place is known in advance.)

Except for the greeting of the head usher, there should be as little talking as possible—silence becomes the church. Where a person has no regular place to sit, and has not expressed preference, seating should be so as to keep the congregation well forward and the various sections of the room balanced as to occupancy.

One question arises: should everyone be ushered? The services of an usher should never be pressed upon anyone, but if the usher acts as though this is the honor extended to each, there is little likelihood that many will refuse to be led to a seat.

A second question: when should the calendars or bulletins be handed to the person being seated? As has been said, the head usher should be freed of this task, so the duty falls upon the ushers inside the church. The best time seems to be just as the person is entering the pew. If there is a group of two or more, the usher may find it best to give the last of the group the calendars for the entire party.

After the responsibility of seating, the next important function of the ushers is the reception of the offering. Nothing in church services varies more than the method of taking up the offering. Before the hour of worship, the head usher, or someone appointed, should check on the offering plates to make sure they are in the proper place and in sufficient numbers. In some churches the plates are at the front of the church for the pastor to hand to the ushers or for the ushers to pick up for themselves. Prayer may be offered before the collection or after. Sometimes the custom is to return the plates to the front, and sometimes the custom is to keep them at the back to be given to the persons charged with counting and recording the money. The ushers must be familiar with the customs in use. Also, if there is a guest speaker who is to preside over the service, the head usher should confer with that person to make sure that there is to be no change in the regular routine.

Just before the time of the offering, the ushers will come quietly to the aisle down which they are to march. The head usher will not be involved in the actual receiving of the offering but will remain at the rear of the church to direct everything. If the offering is taken fairly early in the service, one usher should be appointed to remain at the entrance to receive any latecomers and to request them to wait until the ushers are through with the offering.

Promptness in being assembled to march down the aisle at a signal given by the pastor or organist can be a great virtue in ushering. Marching two by two should be as quiet as possible. If no provision has been made for organ or choral music during the offering, the head usher might suggest this to the pastor. While the plates are being passed through the pews, no usher should speak to a person in the congregation. Shortcuts made by extending the plate across the laps of several people should be avoided. It is far better to pass the plate all the way through the pew or to have an usher at each end to cover a half of the pew. If the plate is passed completely from one end of a pew to another, the receiving usher will start the same plate in the opposite direction at each alternate pew.

If the offering is to be returned to the front of the church, the head usher will see to it that the ushers are ready to march at the signal from the pastor or at the first note of the Doxology. After the plates are handed to the pastor or placed on a table, the ushers should return as a group to the rear of the church, not falling out at their family pews. After reaching the rear, each one may quietly return to sit with the family, or the body of ushers may occupy a reserved pew at the back of the church. If the offering is left at the rear of the church, the head usher should be responsible for it until it is received by the treasurer or other officer.

A third task of the ushers is that of registration. One usher, or several as needed, should have the task of counting the people and recording the result in whatever book is provided. This count will be of value to the church clerk, perhaps, and should become part of the ushers' permanent records. Strangers should be invited to sign the guest book. Cards to be filled in by strangers or visitors should be kept in the pews. The pastor may wish to announce a time for such registration, and a notice might be in the calendar. Great value is attached to this, since registration provides a record of nonmembers who may be in need of the church's ministry or who may be prospective members.

There are other tasks to keep an usher from being idle! He or she should watch over the ventilation, draw curtains to keep sun glare out of the eyes of the attendants, check the thermostat during the heating season, and know where the first aid kit is located in the event of an emergency. At least one usher should watch for any signals from the pastor indicating some need in the congregation or some adjustment to lights, heat, or other physical conditions. If there is something the pastor should know, an usher may write the information on a small slip of paper and hand it to the pastor at the time of the offering or in an unobtrusive way at some other point in the service.

The report of the head usher at the annual meeting will include attendance and registration information and a list of the regular and substitute ushers who have served during the year, with a becoming word of gratitude for their helpfulness.

If any further word may be given to an ushering committee, it might be: suggest becoming attire according to the custom of the church being served; encourage the ushers to enter into the spirit of worship; strive to make the ushering a real asset to the services of the church.

The Pulpit (Search) Committee.

There are two general philosophies concerning a pulpit committee (or search committee). The first is that such a committee is required only when the pulpit is vacant and a new pastor must be found. Churches following this procedure will elect the committee at a special meeting and for the period of time necessary to choose the new minister.

The other way of looking at the pulpit committee is from the wider angle of a year-round service. Churches holding to this custom will elect a pulpit committee annually, and this committee will serve for one year. No church knows when there will be a pastoral change, and the theory is that the committee is to acquaint itself with the pastoral function and to be available to the pastor for any help that may be given. Such help would involve locating pulpit supplies during the minister's vacation, illness, or other absence. Some churches give this complete responsibility to the pulpit committee, while others ask that the committee secure approval of the pulpit supplies from the deacons (see the section on the deacons). There are some real advantages to the standing type of pulpit committee. The members of it receive some training in the ways pastors are found and in the pastor's duties. Also, if the pulpit should become vacant suddenly—as by the pastor's death—the emergency situation can be cared for with no delay.

Let us now consider the tremendous responsibility that this committee carries when a new pastor must be found.

Whether an annual committee or a special committee, the pulpit committee charged with locating a pastor will follow the same routine, except that the annual committee will have informed itself on the procedure, whereas the special committee must make this study the first item on its agenda. With an elected chairperson and secretary, the committee is ready to face the task. Usually it is agreed that meetings will be held at the call of the chairperson.

First, the committee may ask, "How shall we secure names of capable, worthy, available candidates?" There will be names that come unsolicited. The news of the vacant pulpit will be spread by the church membership, by the press, by denominational papers, and in other ways. Pastors of other churches will have their names submitted by friends; members of the congregation will have heard "good preachers" who should be considered; pastors desiring a change may present their own names. Only when there is an exceptional circumstance should the names of self-submitted candidates be given a second thought. Pastors who are doing a creditable work and whose character is good can always arrange for their names to be included on an "available" list filed with the denominational offices. Rarely will a pulpit committee find the list of unsolicited names at all adequate for their search.

On its own initiative, then, the committee will gather names. The state denominational executive, a city executive, and—of prime importance—the national denominational agency that has an accumulation of the profiles of most of the ministers in active service is prepared to assist a church by presenting names of possible candidates for the pulpit. The deans or placement secretaries of seminaries can be of great help, although it will be understood that they will put forward graduates of their own schools.

To the list of the unsolicited and the list of solicited names might be added the names of ministers who have supplied the pulpit at one time or another and who were well received by the church. The author of a book or an article that has attracted attention may have the necessary qualifications. In several ways, then, the list of names before the committee will grow to usable proportions.

Once the list is large enough, the committee will go over it painstakingly. A number of names, for various reasons, will not survive the first examination. The names left after the first go-around will merit further investigation. If complete records have not been obtained for all of these names, this lack should be made up immediately. And, in order to avoid waste of time, effort, and false expectation, the committee should learn definitely which of the names represent pastors who are *available*. To work ethically and with Christian fellowship, the committee should not go out to tempt a pastor to leave his present field. The kind of pastor a church needs is one who has come to the conclusion that, under God's guidance, he or she may make a change without doing harm to his or her present work.

Looking at a pastor's profile, a committee will take note of:
- length of service in the present church
- the types of services considered to be strengths (such as preaching, pastoral calling, evangelism, etc.)
- family situation
- present salary considerations
- reasons given for being willing to make a change
- achievements in present and former churches

Age, sex, and race should not be items of prejudice as the committee does its work. To find the person God has prepared for the task is the one great object of the committee.

Names that appear favorable to the committee will next be compared to the profile of the ideal pastor that the committee has drawn up (usually by soliciting the help of the church members, who may use forms for this that are available from denominational sources).

With a few names put at the top of the list, the committee is ready to begin the work of selection. The time-honored (if not the best) way is for members of the committees to visit the church a pastor is serving to observe and listen. Before making such a trip, the committee must ascertain the hour of service and the street location of the church. Again, the time-honored way is to do this secretly so that the candidate will be taken unaware in order that the sermon heard and the service observed will be as representative as possible. Unless the pulpit committee is small, it is customary for part of the committee to hear a pastor and report to the others, especially if the church served is not so large that strangers might be spotted.

After several pastors are heard, it is likely that one will seem to be outstanding. If not all of the committee have heard this candidate, it may be wise for those who have not observed to be sent to confirm the committee's decision. At this time it is wise to have a conference with the pastor following the service to make sure that he or she would be willing to have his or her name submitted to the church in need. If the pastor is willing to make an investigation, an appointment will be made for a visit to the home church to look over the building, parsonage (if any), and community. Then the candidate will meet with the committee to see if there can be agreement on both sides. If there is a meeting of the minds, a date will be set for the candidate to occupy the pulpit as the choice of the committee recommended to the church.

Before the pastor comes for a formal appearance in the pulpit, it will be wise to send out a biographical sketch to the congregation about two weeks in advance. A coffee hour or other informal event might be planned following the service to permit the members to speak to the candidate and become acquainted.

After the candidate is heard, the pulpit committee should request that the moderator call a special meeting of the church as soon as possible to vote on the person presented. If the vote is favorable, it is a courtesy for the committee to telephone the candidate to apprise him or her of the action. A check will be made, also, to make sure that the church clerk sends a confirming letter without delay. If the vote is unfavorable, a letter with a full explanation should go out immediately.

There are two important things for the committee to bear in mind: (1) Just as soon as the committee has decided on a candidate to present and that person has agreed, the complete financial arrangements should be clearly stated: salary, fringe benefits, housing, moving expenses, and so forth. (2) The sacred word of the candidate should be secured that, if the church extends a call, the call will be accepted.

The custom of playing off one candidate against another, or of giving the congregation a choice among several is so outmoded that it may be a waste of time to mention it. However, if there are any in a church who are accustomed to hearing more than one candidate in the pulpit and then having the entire slate presented for vote at the meeting to call the pastor, they should be informed that this is an old method— and a cruel one—that is no longer practiced widely. One should be considered at a time. Only if the first one fails to be called should another candidate be brought before the church. The committee may have a second choice if the first is not acceptable, but only the committee will know the identity of this person until that one is brought to preach.

A special pulpit committee will have no report to make to

the church other than the presentation of the candidate; an annual pulpit committee will report at the annual meeting concerning any work that may have been done.

Other Committees

The four committees discussed above are common to most churches of a congregational polity, but beyond these four there will be a wide divergence of custom. Some of the other committees frequently found will be examined now.

1. *The baptismal committee.* A baptismal committee often is constituted by the deacons and is composed of both men and women. The committee has the oversight of the baptismal robes, making sure that they are clean and available when needed. In Baptist and in some other churches, the candidates may wear their own clothing, but the trend is for them to wear an outer robe provided by the church. When the pastor has informed the committee of the candidates for baptism, the committee will be in touch with these persons and will fit a robe to each. These robes will be marked with the names of the candidates and will be placed in the space set apart for dressing. At the time of baptism, a deacon or deacons will be in or near the dressing room to assist the candidate if necessary—women for the women and girls, men for the men and boys. Assistance often is welcomed when the candidate comes back wet from the pool.

Inasmuch as baptism is considered a symbol of a spiritual experience, the committee will do everything possible to keep the procedure one of reverence and quiet joy.

This committee is under the jurisdiction of the deacons.

2. *The evangelism committee.* This committee will plan, foster, and carry out the evangelistic efforts of the church, bearing in mind that all that a Christian church does must have an evangelistic basis. This committee may be given the task of drawing up and presenting to the church a year's plan for specific evangelistic outreach. If the denomination, or other group, calls for cooperation in a joint evangelism program, this committee should be prepared to study the suggestions and make recommendations to the church. Prayer groups to undergird the evangelistic efforts may be sponsored by this committee. The committee may be a church-elected group or may be a subcommittee of the deacons. In any event, it works closely with the deacons.

3. *The missions committee.* While the work of missions education is definitely part of the task of the board of Christian education, many churches feel that it is helpful to have a missions committee with the chief function of keeping the work of missions in the forefront of the church's outlook. This committee may advise the budget committee on appropriations for international missions, national missions, and community missions. In churches where there is a missions, ministries, or missionary (all names are used, we find) committee, great care should be taken that there is no overlapping of responsibility or activity where several groups take a substantial interest in the work that is beyond the parish.

4. Committees having to do with the work of deacons, trustees, board of Christian education, and the church school will be covered in the reports on those groups. For work of other committees, such as stewardship, help may be found by

applying to denominational agencies, such as the Division of World Mission Support.

Helpful Books for Further Investigation

Johnson, Alvin D., *The Work of the Usher*. Valley Forge: Judson Press, 1966.

Sawyer, David R., *Work of the Church: Getting the Job Done in Boards and Committees*. Valley Forge: Judson Press, 1987.

Chapter 3

Deacons and Clerk

What Is in a Name?

The office of the one we call pastor, minister, or preacher is referred to in the New Testament by words that are translated bishop, presbyter, or elder. There is no indication at all that there is a gradation in the pastoral office—the words appear to have been used synonymously as far as scholars are able to determine. When we find, then, that Paul, writing to Timothy in the words found in the third chapter of First Timothy, makes a distinction between bishop and deacon, we infer that two separate offices are being discussed. Inasmuch as we know that, in that context, bishop means pastor, we suppose that deacon refers to a person engaged in the work given to the seven chosen by the apostles to aid them in the distribution of alms and in visitation. In any event, deacon is the name long given to a person who does work such as that set forth in the sixth chapter of the Acts. This office, call it by whatever name you will, is the only one established in the early church, with the exception of pastor. All other offices appear to have had a later origin. For this reason, the deacon holds an important and essential office in the church.

The Board of Deacons

The board of deacons has a presiding officer who may be elected by the board or who may come into the position by seniority (in those churches not practicing rotation of the office). In this latter case he may be known as the senior deacon. The board selects one of the number as secretary; there may be a treasurer also. Some boards prefer to keep their transactions oral and off the record, although there are acts that deserve to be recorded for future reference.

1. *The number of deacons*. Because the account in Acts 6 of what we take to be the first deacons gives seven as the number selected, some churches hold to the custom of having seven and no more, although this is becoming rarer as time goes on. We may think it likely that the first deacons were appointed to care for certain divisions by nationalities, by districts of the city, or by special responsibilities. The number is not sacred and was not intended as a precedent. For the most part, churches follow the basic principle found in Acts 6 and elect deacons as necessary for the work to be done. Surely, a church of two thousand members needs a larger corps of deacons than a church of two hundred or fewer. The error is usually on the short side, which results in loading too much work on each member. In a small church there should be a deacon for each twenty-five members; a large church should plan for not fewer than a number that allows one

deacon for each fifty members. Perhaps a good minimum would be five deacons for a small church and seven to twelve for a larger church. The church constitution should make provisions for increasing the size of the board of deacons if and when the membership increases.

2. *How chosen*. Deacons are elected by the church at its annual meeting except that in the case of a vacancy by reason of death or resignation the office may be filled by action at a special meeting or in some other manner carefully spelled out in the constitution. This office is one that should not be filled haphazardly or hurriedly, but with due deliberation and with careful consideration of the merits of the candidates.

3. *Term of office*. A pastor is called for an indefinite period, and other officials are elected, usually, for a specified term, but the time of service for deacons varies. For many years, Baptist churches held to the custom of electing deacons for a life term. This grew out of the ritual of setting apart the ones chosen by a form of ordination. Inasmuch as it was felt that an ordination could not be set aside at an annual meeting, the saying "Once a deacon, always a deacon" became common. Some churches continue on this life-term basis, either with or without an ordination. However, the majority of churches now elect deacons with a prescribed term of office. The preferred arrangement seems to be a term of three years, with eligibility for reelection only after one year out of office. There are several good reasons for this limited term of office: a candidate who appeared to have all the qualifications for the trust at the time of election may turn out to be unworthy or incapable of the responsibilities; deaths and resignations are

so few that a life-term board may see few or no changes for five to ten years at a time, which may mean that the same set of people will tend to a status quo attitude; there will be no room for new people with splendid possibilities for the office—people who have come from elsewhere or who have grown up in the church. A limited tenure permits the removal of the less fit, avoids hard feelings, and guarantees the church the opportunity for utilizing the best of the younger and newer people within the membership.

There are occasions when a life-term deacon grows old or suffers ill health and can no longer be active. The church may then relieve that one of responsibilities and honor the person with the title of deacon emeritus. A deacon on a limited term may be reelected several times and be so worthy of affection and gratitude that that one is made a life deacon with the privilege of attending the meetings of the deacons if that is the wish.

Churches with the life-term plan elect a deacon only when there is a vacancy.

4. *Qualifications*. For qualifications we turn to verses 8 to 13 in the third chapter of First Timothy. Perhaps nowhere is there a better description of the ideal deacon. The stress is upon character. From this passage of Scripture has emerged the church's picture of a deacon. The candidate must be of high morals, ideals, and practices; of good family life; settled in religious faith; an example-setter and inspirer to others in the church.

Added to character, we ask that one be willing and able to give time to the task. A saint who is so busy that little time can be spared for the work of the board is of little value.

The constitution of some churches sets a minimum age for a deacon. Maturity has been thought to be a requisite for this job. Experience has shown that flexibility is the better policy. Some people at twenty-one or twenty-five evince more ability and dedication than many who are older. Indeed, many churches now insist that the board have at least one young person included—in some instances of high school age. This is thought to be a representation of the youth in the church and to be a good way of training younger people.

In churches having an associate membership for those who have not been baptized by immersion, the office of deacon may or may not be open to those holding membership on this basis.

5. *Installation.* The good habit of holding a service of recognition and installation of newly elected or appointed officials is growing. Excellent orders of service for this kind of event may be found in service books. In churches working on the limited-term basis, the deacons are included in this service with no distinction beyond that of all the other officers. The life-term deacon receives his or her setting apart, or ordination, once, following soon after election. In any sort of observance of this kind, stress should be laid on both the acceptance of the responsibility by the officials *and* the acceptance of the officials by the congregation.

6. *Duties.* The chief duty of a deacon is that laid upon the seven in the book of the Acts, namely the assistance given to the pastor so that the tasks not requiring special training may be in the hands of the deacons, thus freeing pastoral time for

graver responsibilities. In the early church the tasks of the deacons included the distribution of alms and visitation. Added to these two original jobs, today's deacon finds many others. As we look at some of the duties, it is well to remember that in some churches the board of deacons will take time at the first meeting of the year to assign to each member some particular responsibility.

(*a*) *Assistance with the ordinances.* Too often has it been thought that the most important (and the most prestigious) of the deacon's privileges is that of helping with the Lord's Supper and baptism. This, however, is but a small part of the total job. But it is a function that requires good preparation and understanding. The two ordinances are the outward symbols displayed publicly of two great events.

(1) *The Ordinance of the Lord's Supper.* When Communion is to be served, the preparation of the table and the front of the sanctuary will be in the deacons' hands. The Communion table and the pastor's chair—and the deacons' chairs if they are not to sit in the front pews—should be arranged well before the time of the service. Hymnals, offering plates, and other equipment should be gathered and placed in ample time.

Fresh bread cut in small pieces, or wafers, must be provided in sufficient quantity to care for the estimated number who will partake. If the bread trays are to be covered (and this is in the best tradition), the napkins or doilies should be newly laundered for the occasion. The pastor may prefer to have one piece of bread left uncut in order that he may break it during the ritual. Often a finger bowl is placed at the disposal of the pastor for the cleansing of the fingertips. The water in the bowl should be fresh and the bowl covered with a napkin, which will be used for drying the fingers.

The grape juice must be fresh. The cups or glasses on the trays must be as clean and sterile as possible. When the deacons have prepared the bread and juice, they will arrange the trays and covers with care. The table will have been covered with a clean cloth (usually white). Following the service, the deacons will be responsible for the collecting and washing of the cups.

Before the service, it is well for the serving deacons of the day to hold a briefing meeting, perhaps a short rehearsal, so that each person will know in advance what is to be done and how.

If the pastor is in the habit of serving Communion to the sick and shut-ins later in the day, certain deacons should be appointed to assist. The small Communion kit that will be taken to homes and hospitals must be provided with bread and grape juice. One or more deacons will accompany the pastor in this visitation.

(2) *The Ordinance of Baptism.* The deacons are responsible for the oversight of the baptismal committee as outlined in the report on committees.

(b) *Sponsoring candidates for membership.* Usually persons desiring to unite with the church will make their request known to the pastor, who will arrange a conference with the deacons. Persons who apply for admission to church membership following baptism are instructed by the pastor, usually in membership classes before baptism. After the pastor is satisfied that the candidates are ready for baptism and church membership, they will be brought to a meeting of the deacons. The deacons should question the candidates concerning their reason for requesting baptism, for desiring to join this particular church, their understanding of the meaning of what they are doing, their basic Christian beliefs, etc. And the deacons should welcome questions from the candidates. Some deacons have been known to say, "I have no questions for this young person—after being in the pastor's class, this one may be better qualified to ask me some questions." This attitude is likely to disillusion the candidate who is new in the faith and has approached this meeting with some awe, thinking that the deacons represent the highest in Christian faith. Too, the pastor needs the support of the deacons in approving or disapproving a person for baptism; the pastor may have some reservations but would like to have the opinion of the deacons. This pastor-deacons-candidate meeting has as its prime purpose the wise counseling of the candidate and assistance in the person's spiritual growth.

Some will desire to unite with the church on the strength of their "Christian experience." They may have lost fellowship with the home church by reason of long absence, the closing of the church, or some other circumstance. They cannot apply for a letter of transfer. The deacons will be concerned to ascertain the facts concerning the inability to secure a letter, and to learn why the person thinks that this church will satisfy deep, inner needs and be a place for outward service.

A third class of candidates to be brought before the deacons will be made up of those who can bring letters of transfer from other churches. There will be little for the deacons to inquire about in such instances except to find out what interests the candidates have in the church program and what they did in their former church home. The thought will be to help in building the candidates into the church life.

When the church comes together to vote on the acceptance of the new members (coming by one of the three ways noted), the deacons will report their findings and make a formal recommendation in respect to each candidate. This report and recommendation is of real value since the other members of the church will have had no occasion to learn much about the newcomers. The members can vote fairly and intelligently only after the deacons inform them as to the facts and possibilities.

(c) *Visitation or "watch care."* Beyond and above the more public duties of the deacons, in time involved and possibly in importance, is the oversight of the members of the church. After the board of deacons is made up for the year, the chairperson or senior deacon will secure a list of the membership with addresses and phone numbers from the clerk or church secretary. The chairperson will call a meeting of the board and the pastor, at which time the membership list will be divided among the deacons. If there are three hundred members, for instance, and six deacons, each deacon will receive approximately fifty names as a fair share. If the community is large, a geographical distribution is wise, but in a smaller community matters of family ties, business alliance, and other relationships are important. The aim will be to give each deacon the names of persons who can be served to the best advantage unhandicapped by personal or occupational ties. It is often wise to change the lists each year so that the deacons will be in touch with different people every twelve months. In this way a deacon will become acquainted with a good proportion of the membership during his or her term of office. After the lists are established, three copies of each should be made: one for the deacon, one for the chairperson, and one for the pastor. In this way, if there should be a misfortune in a home in the parish, there will be no doubt as to which deacon may be called upon to go and be of service. After the deacon receives the list for the year, the work will begin.

First, the deacon may decide to write a letter to go to every home on the list. If the deacon feels that help is needed to compose the letter, the pastor will be ready to make suggestions. Personal letters are best, but if the task is large, a mimeographed letter (with the deacon's signature and a few words of personal greeting in the deacon's handwriting) may serve. Here is a sample letter:

Dear (*name or names to be inserted*):

At a recent meeting of our Board of Deacons, of which I am now a member, we were discussing the privileges and obligations of having been elected to this office. We were concerned particularly about the opportunities for being of help to the other members of the church. So we looked over the membership roll and decided that each of us should take a certain number of people and think of them as a group with which to become better acquainted.

I rejoice that your name is on my list, and I look forward to visiting in your home soon, if I may be permitted, so that we can get to know each other better and profit by talking over the work that we do together in our church.

In the meantime, and at all times, I hope that you will feel free to get in touch with me if something occurs in your church relationship or in your family or personal life with which I, or someone else whom you might prefer, could help.

You have my best wishes for a successful year in every way, and especially for a blessed year in your Christian life.

Sincerely,

(It is to be understood, of course, that in dividing the names, a man who is a deacon will not be given the names of single women, or a woman who is a deacon will not be given the names of single men. In fact, it is not a bad idea to suggest that a deacon take along husband or wife when calling.)

About a week after the letter is mailed, the deacon begins the home visitation. The plan will be to cover the list within a year. The visits are best made when every member of the family is likely to be at home. Usually this means some early evening visitation. If the visits disclose facts that the pastor should know (such as illness, unemployment, change of residence, a new baby, a grievance toward the church) these should be relayed in a careful manner. The deacon can do much to aid the church by being a sympathetic interpreter of the church program and the pastor's work. The deacon will find in some homes circumstances that may make it wise to call several times during the year. This will be true of shut-ins and victims of protracted illness.

When the deacon gets to know the people on his or her list

by sight, if he or she has not known them before, he or she should make it a point to be aware of absences on Sunday morning. After a person is absent for three or four consecutive Sundays, the deacon might well do some checking to find out the reason. An exact way of making this check is by the use of registration cards, either on Communion Sundays or every Sunday. Cards printed for this purpose are available from the denominational book stores. It is well to remind the pastor to request this registration at any appropriate time during the service.

New members, as they are added to the church, will be added to the deacons' lists. These additions deserve immediate and active follow-up until they are well established in their new church home.

(*d*) *Pulpit supplies*. The task of supplying the pulpit during the pastor's absence due to illness, vacation, or special work falls to the lot of the deacons unless this responsibility has been assigned to a pulpit committee (see committees). It is customary for the pastor to confer with the deacons before making plans to be absent from the pulpit. And if the pastor is to be present, but a special speaker is to preach the sermon, the deacons should have the privilege of approving such speakers. If the pastor has a choice of persons to occupy the pulpit during absences, the names may be given to the deacons as the pastor's preferences. If the matter of selecting the preachers is left entirely to the deacons, they may have available the names of persons who have supplied acceptably at former times; former pastors are possibilities; denominational executives will be glad to suggest people.

At the time of inviting persons to supply the pulpit, the deacons should be prepared to state the honorarium offered and whether or not expense money will be allowed in addition. This information may be secured from the treasurer, or it may be a standing budgetary item. The deacons should be sure that the check is ready for the preacher before he or she leaves, inasmuch as that person may have advanced personal funds for travel. In addition to stating the financial arrangements, the person coming should be given directions as to how to reach the church. If coming by public transportation, one deacon should be delegated to meet the guest speaker at the airport or station. In ample time before the service, one or more deacons should go over the program and other details with the speaker. Some churches appoint a deacon to sit on the platform with guest preachers for the introduction and any assistance that the speaker may need or request. Should the speaking engagement necessitate an overnight stay or meals, the deacons should arrange for this entertainment.

(e) *Custodians of the Fellowship Fund.* A survey has shown that most Baptist churches have a Fellowship Fund (sometimes known by other names) made up of Communion Sunday offerings. The board of deacons has charge of this fund and determines the distribution. In the constitution and bylaws of some churches there are specifications as to the use of this money; other churches leave the matter entirely to the discretion of their deacons. The use of the fund is confidential, for the most part, and the expenditures will be known to the deacons and pastor only—in fact, some part of the fund often is placed at the disposal of the pastor for giving to the needy without any requirement to report the names of the recipients. Generally, the Fellowship Fund is for emergency use for the needy among the members. Some churches allow more latitude in the use and consider the pleas of people or causes beyond the membership. The church may be asked to approve any large sum, such as the annual gift to the Missionaries and Ministers Benefit Board. Of late years, the Fellowship Fund of churches may have been disbursed for national or world emergencies, such as world relief, flood relief, earthquake victims, and so forth. The deacons, of course, must abide by the instructions of the church, although they may make recommendations for temporary or permanent changes affecting the use of this money. The Fellowship Fund, at all times, must be considered a sacred trust, and the money must be protected against unworthy claimants.

(f) *Board of review*. The board of deacons is called upon occasionally to pass upon the seemliness or advisability of some suggested new activity to be held in a church building. For instance, one municipality requested the use of the church building as a polling place. The pastor, wisely, referred this matter to the deacons. Money-making projects, such as rummage sales, raffles, Bingo, events with paid admission, and similar schemes, should not be scheduled and advertised until the deacons have been given the opportunity to review the implications. Members, of course, who are not satisfied with the action of the deacons may request a hearing at a church meeting. The deacons should not let their own personal prejudices sway their actions; the counsel to the group requesting an unusual use of the building should be governed by the effect upon the whole church. One small group might be made happy and be profited by the event while the overall result on the image and work of the church might be on the negative side. The deacons should not leave to the pastor decisions about borderline activities; if the pastor decides either for or against what is being promoted, there are bound to be some members who will disagree with the judgment, and this may lessen the pastor's influence for good. If the deacons make an unpopular decision, the members must admit that an elected board was fulfilling proscribed duties in a democratic fashion.

(g) *Pastor's acolytes.* The word "acolyte" is not used widely in Baptist churches, but it expresses what is meant here. While the deacons have no special ecclesiastical powers, the office of deacon is honored by the church in a sense that no other office is. Thus, the deacons have a nearness to the pastor that suggests doing whatever may be done to encourage and help with the work. Small things, such as checking the pulpit and the platform before the service, arranging for a glass of water near at hand if the pastor finds this helpful, helping the pastor don the robe (if a robe is worn), and *meeting in the study for prayer before the service* may do much to let the pastor know that the deacons are supportive and earnestly desiring that the service be a spiritual high point. The pastor's wishes, of course, must be respected; each pastor has ways of doing things; one may feel greatly lifted by having the deacons at hand while another may wish to be alone. In any event, an established relationship of mutual respect and helpfulness between deacons and pastor can do much toward guaranteeing the progress of the mutual task.

(h) *Responsibility for "spiritual" phases of the work.* Looked at carefully, the total work of any church cannot be divided into "spiritual" and "material" areas. The function of the church is proclamation and mission. Even though a church must have tangible tools, such as building and equipment and money, to do its work, there is no reason for thinking of the work of the officials responsible for these tools as secondary to that of the deacons. Nevertheless, the actual face-to-face, personal witnessing often is thought of as the spiritual side of the work, and the deacons may be assigned to this phase of the activity. In the job description of deacons, churches may include leading the church in its evangelistic emphases. If there is an evangelism committee (see Committees) it may be a subcommittee of the deacons or be appointed by the deacons. Where this responsibility is placed upon the deacons, the board will work with the pastor in planning the year's program of outreach and will consider denominational programs of this kind. Whether rightly or wrongly, churches look to the deacons to lead the church in its God-appointed task of bringing the unconverted into a saving relationship with the Christ. If the deacons are passive in this regard, the church is likely to be passive.

Deaconesses

If a church retains the title "deaconess," the constitution will provide for the election of women to this office in much the same way as deacons are selected.

More and more churches have come to the point of making

up the board of deacons of both men and women with no distinction of function or privilege.

For the benefit of churches that do maintain two separate boards—deacons and deaconesses—it may be said that the traditional duties of the deaconess include parish visitation, the preparation of the Communion materials, washing the Communion cups, assisting candidates at the time of baptism, helping individuals or families in need.

Where there is this separate board of deaconesses, the meetings will be held as a board and not with the deacons, except that there may be joint meetings from time to time. If a husband is on one board and his wife on the other, the two may collaborate in the calling program with real profit.

Junior Deacons

A board of junior deacons is found in some churches. Young people are elected to this office for the purpose of training for later responsibilities. In churches where the board of deacons includes both men and women, the junior deacons include both sexes; in churches where there are two boards, there will be two junior boards.

Junior deacons may be asked to appear on the church platform to take some part in the morning service; they may assist with the ushering; they may be asked to attend the meeting of the deacons as auditors from time to time; they may be assigned the task of calling in the homes of people of their own age.

In a few churches, the junior deacons are people from the ages of eighteen to thirty-five who have the same privileges as the regular deacons. The chief advantage of such a board is to give opportunity to more people to get a taste of the deacon's work. This is especially helpful in a large church where there are many members to be served. The disadvantage of this more mature board of junior deacons is that it automatically sets the age for the regular deacons at thirty-six plus and tends to make the board on the older side. The experience of many churches is that more is to be gained by having young people on the regular board.

The Clerk

The clerk is elected at the annual meeting of the church, for a one-year term. The office, however, is one having no bar to reelection. Inasmuch as the qualifications for clerk are special and the work is of a continuing nature, a good clerk may be kept for a decade or longer. A clerk who has served for a number of years becomes a valuable resource on matters of membership, church statistics, and trends in church life.

In order to be effective, the clerk must be able to present legible records in longhand or typing; a knowledge of simple bookkeeping is helpful; characteristics of patience and promptness are desirable; and *accuracy* is of the utmost importance. Beyond these qualifications, the clerk should be a person who has the respect of the church and the community, inasmuch as the church will expect the clerk to represent the members in many public affairs. The clerk usually has the following duties:

1. *Keeping the minutes.* The clerk must be present, or arrange for a substitute to be present, at all regular and special

meetings of the church. In some instances the clerk will be asked to serve as secretary of special committees or boards that make their minutes a part of the church records. The clerk will make an accurate record of the proceedings of these church meetings and later inscribe the minutes in a permanent record book provided by the church. This record book must be kept in such a way that the contents will be readable by future generations. Often this book is used in courts to establish facts necessary to a transaction or litigation involving the church or a member. At meetings of the church, the clerk will read "the minutes of the last meeting." This may seem a boring part of a meeting to the uninitiated, but it is a vital part because it confirms actions that have been taken and discloses "unfinished business" that must not be neglected.

2. *Implementing the minutes.* As a church meeting proceeds, there may be committees appointed. Some of the appointees may be present; others may not be present. However, even if all appointees are present, the clerk will notify each person of the responsibility and the duties expected, together with any other information, such as date of report, and so on. This notification will be in writing and the clerk will keep a copy for the files. In fact, the clerk is required to keep a copy of all letters that are written on behalf of the church. In addition to letters of reminder to elected or appointed officials, a clerk may be authorized to write letters of condolence, thanks, expostulation, or inquiry. In addition to letters and appointments, the clerk may be called upon to request a chairperson of a board or committee to follow through on an action passed by the church. Some officials

may refuse to go ahead on an important issue until the receipt of an official letter from the clerk that will be proof of authority. It is customary for copies of the minutes of a church meeting to be sent to the pastor and the moderator (unless the pastor serves as moderator). At times, the clerk may need to pick out items of unfinished business and refer these to the person or persons responsible for taking action on the items or for preparing recommendations for the church.

3. *Keeping the church roll.* If any one task of the clerk is more important than all others, it is the keeping of the church roll. The members are the church, and only by an accurate record of the names and addresses of the members can a church be kept an efficiently functioning unit. Even in small communities, or in small churches in large communities, the turnover of the membership is surprisingly high. The pastor and clerk can be mutually helpful by reporting to each other all changes that come to their attention. The church roll is the basis for all mailings of literature by the church; it provides the list for any financial canvass; it is necessary to the deacons for the preparation of their calling lists; it is the resource for people in the church who need to approach others according to age or sex groupings; associational dues are assessed according to this roll; denominational statistics are gathered from church rolls. Indeed, a membership roll to which have been added all new members to date and from which have been removed the names of members who are deceased, who have moved, or who have been stricken from membership for one reason or another, that shows up-to-the-minute addresses, changes in names due to marriage, and so forth,

is an invaluable asset to any church. The whole responsibility for the existence of such a roll falls on the clerk.

The clerk will keep the roll in such a way as to indicate active and inactive members (where a church recognizes this division), resident and nonresident members, and regular and associate members (in churches where these designations are used). Some churches have what are known as constituent members, that is, people who attend and contribute to the church but who do not join. All divisions of membership recognized by the church served must be clearly marked on the roll by the clerk.

The church roll may be kept in a permanent roll book or stored in a computer. If the clerk does not use a computer, an index-card file is a useful supplement. Card files and computer entries both should contain the following information: date on which the person joined the church; date of baptism if the person was baptized in this church; age, if known; date of death or removal when such information must be recorded; and, if the removal is by letter of transfer, the date of the letter and the name of the church requesting it must be recorded. This information is valuable not only to the church but also in legal matters, such as the issuance of birth certificates, passports, the settling of estates, and the like. It is also possible that families may find help in these records for tracing ancestry.

4. *Custodian of the records*. In addition to the book of minutes and the files, the clerk will be in charge of the records of past years, of deeds and titles, of such minutes of church organization as seem worthy of a permanent place in the

church history, and of the seal of the church. Sometimes there is a church charter to be kept in a safe place. The clerk will determine which of these records are of real value to the church and will make sure that they are carefully placed in a safe-deposit box, in a fireproof safe, or other good location. Some states have an archives department that will receive old records that have historical value; usually such a department will return photographed copies of these records to the church. The denomination, also, has a historical society serving churches in this way.

5. *Announcements and publicity.* The charter or constitution of a church usually provides that a notice of church meetings be mailed to members, posted in the church bulletin, or announced from the pulpit a specified number of days before the meeting. This is another of the clerk's duties. If the clerk fails in this, a meeting may need to be postponed. When a meeting is held without full notification, actions taken have no standing and may be declared null and void.

6. *Preparation of reports.* It is a common practice for churches to prepare an annual report consisting of reports from all church groups detailing their activities for the previous year. The clerk's role is to prepare a report showing the membership status: additions, losses, deaths, and the present total. The clerk will file a copy of this report with the Association and the other denominational groups involved. The clerk will fill out a report as required by any of these bodies. If a government agency needs any information that a church is willing to give, the clerk will be asked to fulfill the request.

7. *Dismissal of members.* Forms for the transfer or dismiss-

al of members will be kept in stock by the clerk. The church may procure these from a denominational bookstore, or may have an individual form printed. (Some churches prefer to write a personal letter rather than use a form.) Whenever a member requests a transfer by letter to some other church and the request is granted by the church, the clerk will fill out the proper form and mail it to the clerk or pastor of the other church. Usually there is a stub on the form, which is to be returned to the clerk after the other church has added the member to its roll. If this acknowledgment is not received in due time, the clerk should write a letter of inquiry. Theoretically, the member remains a member of the home church until notice has been received of reception into the other church. Likewise, when a person requests membership in the church served by the clerk a letter must be secured before membership is granted.

Helpful Books for Further Investigation

Grenell, Zelotes, and Goss, Agnes Grenell, *The Work of the Clerk*. Valley Forge: Judson Press, 1967.

Nichols, Harold, *The Work of the Deacon and Deaconess*. Valley Forge: Judson Press, 1965, 1984.

Torbet, Robert G., *A History of the Baptists*. 3rd. ed. Valley Forge: Judson Press, 1973.

Chapter 4

Financial Officers

No Second-Rate Church Officers

The humblest bit of work done for a church has a definite spiritual content; therefore, it is incorrect to divide church tasks into two realms—the spiritual and the material. In other words, it is straying from the real facts to state bluntly that the deacons are in charge of the "spiritual" concerns of the church, while the trustees handle only the material concerns. Nevertheless, a church does have assets that are material in the eyes of the law. These are the real estate (church buildings and, often, a parsonage), movable equipment of various kinds, funds invested in stocks and bonds or on deposit in banks, and cash on hand. The deacons have designated functions that keep them busy. There must also be officers to take the burden of safeguarding the tangibles of the church. This report will deal chiefly with the business officers of the church.

The Board of Trustees

The common term for the group of people elected to care for the property of a church is "board of trustees." Some churches prefer the term "stewards." If a church is incorporated (a highly desirable procedure), the title of trustee may be designated in the charter granted to a church so that the church has little choice. The title is of little consequence; trustees are stewards in any event. As stewards they hold in trust for the church membership the material possessions that have accrued to the church. An autonomous church, such as a Baptist church, holds full title to all property that is donated to it or purchased by it. Of course, the church has the inalienable right to vote on the disposition of its assets, but to comply with the laws and to be assured of skilled administration of assets, it is necessary to empower representatives to hold property, to administer it, and to handle all legal and financial details concerning it. The trustees have these responsibilities and others that the church may delegate to them. For ordinary administration the members of the board are competent, by granted powers, to act on their own initiative; on all unusual matters the church members must vote.

1. *The number of trustees*. The number of trustees is often smaller than the number of deacons in a church. The deacons deal with people, but the trustees deal with property and figures. Even in a very large church the board need not be large, except for the advantage of utilizing the advice of a number of able people. Most frequently found is a board of from five to seven persons.

2. *How elected*. The trustees are elected, customarily, by

the church at its annual meeting, and by classes, as are the deacons in churches using the rotating system. That is to say that a third of the board go out of office each year and, usually, the ones going off stay out of office for one year at least. (It may be said that some churches do not require this one year vacation for the trustees, as is true of deacons, since trustees are selected from among the astute people in the church with experience and ability in handling property and money.) By having one-third of the board elected each year, there is a carry-over of experienced trustees to break in the new people.

3. *Qualifications*. The character and devotion of a trustee should equal that of a deacon, for the trustee is in charge of that which has been bought or given by dedicated people; much of the property represents the result of church offerings and special fund drives. The trustee should be a person of scrupulous honesty combined with practicality, thriftiness (not stinginess!), financial ability, and good judgment. A working knowledge of law is of great benefit. A gem of a trustee is one who is demonstrating these qualities in a business or profession—and certainly in the money matters at home.

4. *Duties*. As has been said, the trustees hold the property of the church in trust. Signatures of certain officers on the board are required on all deeds, transfers of stock, bank notes, mortgages, and checks. Ordinarily, the personal property of trustees is not assessable or involved in any failure of the church to make good on a note or other obligation. It is well for trustees to have legal advice (perhaps there will be a lawyer in the church) to define the extent of their responsibil-

ity before a large obligation is undertaken. The titles to all real estate, stocks and bonds, cash, and other church assets are in their keeping. They receive and disburse moneys for the church. If the church is named as beneficiary in a will, the proceedings for receiving the inheritance will be arranged by the trustees. Unless the will stipulates the exact use of the bequest, the trustees will advise the church concerning the use to which it may be put to advantage.

Disbursements ordered by the church will be made by the trustees. They will give an account to the church annually, or more often, as required. A detailed report of receipts and expenditures, dormant funds, and pieces of real estate will be submitted to the church with regularity. The ability to make such reports involves the keeping of books and other records.

The trustees will endeavor to maintain or improve the property placed in their care. If there are funds invested in stocks and bonds they will keep a careful watch of the records of the companies in which the money is invested and will advise the church when it seems wise to sell or hold. *If a company is involved in some activity that is against the conscience of the church*, the trustees may ask for advice. (For example, companies may be guilty of unfair hiring practices, may refuse to do what can be done to lessen air pollution, may do things to encourage war or violence abroad.) The trustees will arrange for all minor repairs to church property, and will advise major repairs when necessary.

5. *The composition of the board.* Some churches elect trustees and give them the right of deciding in their meetings the responsibility that each trustee is to carry. Other churches

elect trustees, a treasurer of the church, perhaps a financial secretary, and as many assistants as may be required. A finance committee and a budget committee may be elected by the church. In addition, a special committee for the annual pledge drive may be elected—Every Member Enlistment Committee, Every Member Canvass Committee, Church Support Program Committee, or whatever name is preferred by the church. In any event, all of these financial officers are related to the board of trustees either as regular members or as *ex officio* members. All of the responsibilities intermesh to the extent that no individual or committee can work effectively independent of the others. Since the pledging committee usually has other members in addition to financial officers, its relationship to the trustees may be of a consulting nature.

Other Financial Officers

1. *Treasurer.* The treasurer of a church holds one of the most important posts. Rarely does this person receive the amount of gratitude due for the amount of time and thought put into the work. This is accounted for to a large extent by the fact that the treasurer is the one who must remind the members of the need to keep pledges up-to-date, to pay in advance when going on vacation, and to take a rightful share in any emergencies. Also, the treasurer often must refuse to appropriate money for popular causes or demands when the condition of the liquid assets indicates that such expenditure is unwise. The treasurer has several well-defined duties.

(a) *Custodian of liquid assets.* While the board of trustees has oversight of the long-range financing of the church, the

treasurer devotes much of his time to the immediate financing. The offering placed on the plates at services and the
checks that come through the mail go to the treasurer for
deposit. The treasurer knows the balance on hand and, by
referring to the budget, can determine whether or not the
funds are coming in at the necessary rate. If a deficit is
threatened, the treasurer will make the church aware of this
fact before the situation becomes serious.

(b) *Paymaster*. All bills incurred by the church go to the
treasurer for payment. In the budget are the fixed items, such
as salaries, fuel, upkeep, etc. The treasurer will check each
bill to make sure that it covers any expense authorized by the
budget adopted by the church. The salaries, utilities, and other
regular expenses may be paid by the treasurer without authori-
zation other than the budget, but all other bills should be
referred to the one who has contracted the expense or made
the purchase. This is a wise and customary precaution. If the
treasurer detects a bill that is not a budgetary item, that
exceeds the budgetary allotment, or that has not been authorized in a church meeting, this bill should be brought before
the trustees or church before being paid. In smaller churches,
the treasurer will be able to regulate the expenditures because
of having a full knowledge of the church intent, but in larger
churches there may be a large number of people with power
to charge things to the church accounts and this complicates
the task. To a great extent, the credit standing of a church in
the community will depend upon the quality of the treasurer's
work. The promptness with which bills are paid, and the
insistence on holding the church within its financial abilities

determine the financial reputation of the church. This has a spiritual and ethical value: a defaulting, almost bankrupt, church cannot impress a community favorably.

(c) *Banker*. Even in the smallest communities, a church treasurer will have banking facilities available nearby. Payment by check is the wisest custom, and cash payments should be made only in emergencies. If a cash payment is made, the treasurer is within his or her rights to insist on a receipt at the time of payment. Even though the church may have every confidence in the integrity of the treasurer, that person should have, for his or her own protection and satisfaction, some sort of voucher (bill, receipt, cancelled check, etc.) for every cent paid out. The church check book is the exclusive responsibility of the treasurer. If the church authorizes a loan from the bank on recommendation of the trustees, it is usually the treasurer's job to care for the details and to make the payments on the note as due. If the current expense balance is large enough at certain times of the year to warrant placing a part in a savings account, the treasurer will do this.

(d) *Bookkeeper*. The treasurer must keep, or cause to be kept, accurate records of the receipts and expenditures. In addition to the current funds records, there will be records of trust funds, special funds, real estate, and other investments. Reports to the church will be made monthly in addition to the full report at the annual meeting. The trustees must be aware of the church assets.

2. *Assistant Treasurer*. Only large churches find it necessary to have one or more assistant treasurers, insofar as the work is concerned, but the smallest church would be well

advised to have an assistant treasurer so that the work may go on during the illness or absence of the treasurer. Also, if the treasurer should die while in office, there would be an assistant who would know how to pick up the task immediately. The assistant treasurer is not only in the position of a standby but also takes an active part in counting money, verifying figures for the treasurer, being present at times when two signatures may be required on a check or other document. The assistant treasurer may be utilized to help draw up the reports for the church.

3. *Financial Secretary.* In small churches the treasurer may be able to care for the work of the financial secretary and make it unnecessary to elect two persons. But a medium-sized or large church finds it helpful to have a financial secretary. One of the chief tasks of the secretary is to record the payment on members' pledges and to count the loose offering. After the pledges are received during the annual canvass, the secretary will make up a books, card, or computer file showing the name and amount of the pledge. After the Sunday offerings have been received and the treasurer or financial secretary has removed the money from the envelopes and noted the amounts on the envelopes, the financial secretary will take the empty envelopes and record the amounts paid against pledges.

In some churches, the financial secretary takes charge of the offerings and checks the money. After this has been done, the bag of cash and checks is given to the treasurer with a slip showing the amount. Sometimes the secretary goes so far as to make the bank deposit, and then the treasurer receives only the deposit slip. There are several advantages in having the financial secretary handle the money. Many people will mark the amount given on the front of the envelope, and many people will choose not to mark the amount; some will put a double or triple amount in one envelope, having destroyed the others that were not used. With the record of pledges at hand, the secretary can determine how to credit the money. Also, it is easier for the secretary to keep separate the pledge money and the loose offering. Some churches prefer to have both treasurer and secretary work together to avoid error and to share the work load.

The knowledge of the pledges and payments is a confidence honored by the financial secretary.

In many churches there is the custom of sending quarterly statements showing the members how their pledges stand. This is the work of the financial secretary. It is wise to send a statement to everyone who has pledged, even though the pledge is up-to-date. This avoids giving the impression that only the delinquent are being notified. Most members are grateful for the statement, for it calls attention to any mistakes in payment; if the pledge money has been paid in cash, the statement is an acceptable voucher to use for income tax purposes.

A financial secretary may exert a quiet, spiritual influence on the membership by finding opportunities to reinforce the idea of giving in proportion to ability, that is, increasing one's pledge as personal income increases. Good stewardship of material things promotes spiritual growth. Jesus pointed this out by telling his followers that one's heart will be where one's treasure is.

The report of the financial secretary will not be detailed. At the end of the year the secretary will list the total amount pledged, the total amount paid against pledges, and the result. Sometimes the church will request that the pledges be tabulated to indicate how many members pledge and at what level—for instance, how many pledge $2 a week, how many $5, $10, $20, and so on. In such a tabulation, the current expense pledges will be in one column and the mission giving in another unless the church has a unified budget, in which case one pledge covers both projects.

4. *Assistant Financial Secretary.* In churches where the burden of work for the financial secretary is great, an assistant may be elected. Not only does this person share the work but is also in training for larger responsibilities later on.

5. *Treasurers and Secretaries of Missions* (or benevolences). Churches using the duplex envelope plan may prefer to have a separate staff of treasurers and secretaries to handle the benevolence, or missions, money. All money given in the benevolence side of the envelope and all other donations for missions or charity will be turned over to the people handling this fund. The duties of these officers parallel those of the officers handling the current expense. Sometimes the treasurer of the church serves as treasurer of both funds and keeps the money either in separate accounts or in one joint account with careful records available to indicate the amount credited to each fund. The local conditions and personnel available in a church will guide the members in determining how many officials are needed to take proper care of receipts and disbursements.

6. *The Finance Committee*. The finance committee often is a committee of the board of trustees—a group responsible for planning the financing of the church's activities. Unless the church elects separate committees to work on the budget and the Every Member Enlistment Canvass, the finance committee will care for both of these projects. The ongoing work of a finance committee is that of money conservation and investment, while other trustees look to the upkeep of the real estate.

7. *The Budget Committee*. Many churches have come to realize that it is not wise to expect the trustees, finance committee, or regular officials to prepare the annual budget. One reason is that these officials, by the nature of their work, find it necessary to keep down expenses as much as possible and to compare the current year with previous years in various items of the budget. If the church appoints a special budget committee made up of people concerned more with the program of the church and its outreach potentials, they will exercise less inhibited vision and faith and come up with a "dream budget" to challenge the members. This budget may need to be revised after the results of the pledging are known, but it serves to raise the sights of some people and to point out to all members of the congregation the many aspects of the church mission that might be realized by giving in confidence and on a sacrificial level.

The committee will need to recognize, first, whether or not the budget to be drawn up is to be inclusive. The older method of budgeting confined the "church budget" to what are known as "church" expenses and did not take into account the various organizations of the church. The inclusive, or unified, type of budget provides for all branches of church activity, such as the church school, youth activities, women's society, etc. Thus, the budget committee must know which type of budget the church is expecting. If related organizations are to be included, the officers of those organizations will be asked to submit itemized statements of their proposed expenses for the next budget year (showing expected income from other sources, if any).

To arrive at figures for the budget, the committee will start with a copy of the current budget. They will raise questions about whether the salaries of staff—such as pastor, organist, and custodian—will be the same, or should there be increases or reductions? Will the same amount of fuel be needed next year, and has the price changed? Are there items on the current budget that represent temporary emergencies that need not be included this next year? Is it likely that emergency expenses for the coming year will be greater than for this year? The making of a budget entails hard work. There will be comparison; research; consultation with the pastor, other officials, and staff; and close scrutiny of the program outlined for the coming year. One item that must be included is that of "miscellaneous expense" to cover many small, unforeseeable needs.

Once the committee decides on the expenditures on the basis of an irreducible minimum plus a safety margin and has given due attention to what the church ought to be doing in certain fields by inserting larger sums and new appropriations, it will turn to forecasting the probable income to balance the expenses. This income can be expected from pledges, loose offerings at services, interest on bank deposits and investments, and customary gifts from organizations. The one major variable will be the amount of the pledges. After the other income, which can be estimated quite closely, has been totaled, the pledges must be large enough to balance the budget. This amount for pledges is known as the "goal" for the Every Member Enlistment Committee.

A current expense budget will include such items as: salaries, pulpit supplies, pensions and Social Security, parsonage or housing allowance, utilities, office expense, telephone, music, literature for church school and other groups, insurance, contingencies, the organizations (if the budget is inclusive), allowances for normal expenses of officials, etc.

Estimated income projected should include such items as pledges, loose offerings, trust funds (and rentals, if any), organizations' collections, and gifts.

If the budget is unified, one item on it will be outreach, or missions. If separate budgets are in order, the benevolence budget will list the church's share of the unified mission budget of the denomination, special denominational concerns such as the institutional budget, special offerings, donations to interdenominational and community efforts, particular projects adopted by the church through the years. The income will be from pledges designated for benevolences or missions. Sometimes the income from trusts is designated to this part of the church's mission.

One thing to bear in mind is that the first budget presented to the church is tentative, inasmuch as the pledges have not yet been solicited. The budget committee will submit this budget to the trustees, finance committee, or church for provisional approval. After this approval is received, the budget will become the goal for the Every Member Pledging Committee. When the returns from Pledge Sunday and the follow-up have been totaled and allowance has been made for what may come in later, the budget committee will revise the first budget upward or downward to make it balance with the money that can be expected. If the committee has done its work with faith and optimism, the budget must be revised downward in most churches. This soberer and balanced budget will then be submitted to the church, this time for adoption. On occasion, a church will rebel at the cuts that have been necessary and will insist on restoring some or all of them by adopting a "deficit budget." This is wise only if a church has an endowment to fall back upon in case of need, or if the prospects for growth warrant a "go on faith" attitude. A deficit budget can lower morale if the treasurer must appeal to the members for greater giving time after time.

8. *Financial Enlistment Committee*. Through the years this committee has gone by a number of names: Every Member Canvass, Every Member Enlistment, Stewardship, and so on. But, by whatever name it is known to a local church, its chief task has remained the same. That task is two-pronged: to promote a growing sense of stewardship among the members, and to give the members the opportunity for expressing that stewardship by pledging to the expenses of the church, including its world outreach.

The Division of World Mission Support of the American

Baptist Churches is charged with the responsibility "to develop a spirit of beneficence among the constituency." In fulfilling this responsibility, its leaders and staff have sought not only to raise funds for the Baptist World Mission but also to help local churches develop a greater sense of stewardship among their members and thus to provide funds for the total ministry of the church. Baptists have been foremost in the development of tools for carrying out one of the most important projects in the life of a church, that of the annual financial enlistment. Each year, under a capable field staff and with specially trained volunteers, instruction is made available to the pastor and financial leaders of every local church. An inquiry at the state or city office will bring information concerning training sessions in the vicinity of the church. For many years the chief emphasis has been placed on the Every Member Canvass, and up-to-date manuals outlining the most efficient method of conducting such a canvass are available.

If a church utilizes the planned emphasis as outlined in the manuals, the necessity will be seen for a separate Every Member Enlistment Committee, with each member having a special responsibility for conducting the canvass on whatever basis the church decides. The duties of the committee, chiefly, will be to plan for the enlistment, set up the special training committees for the teams that are to go out, arrange for the publicity materials and the pledge cards, conduct the enlistment on the day or week set aside, and carry through to completion this part of the church's work. The committee will have its work done only when the enlistment is completed insofar as possible, and the results are handed over to the budget committee, financial secretary, or whoever the church decides should make a record of the pledges received. (As has been said before, it is wise to keep this information confidential, and the financial secretary usually is the one who sees the pledges that come in.)

If the church does not use the manuals made available by the denominational offices, or any other guidance material, the committee will need to do some substantial work on its own in studying methods and ways and means of conducting the annual enlistment for funds for the program of the church. It is usually considered unwise, however, for the committee to go on its own, inasmuch as so much helpful material is readily available.

Helpful Books for Further Investigation

McLeod, Thomas E., *The Work of the Church Treasurer, revised*. Valley Forge: Judson Press, 1992.

Tibbetts, Orlando F., *The Work of the Church Trustee*. Valley Forge: Judson Press, 1979.

Van Benschoten, A.Q., Jr., *What the Bible Says About Stewardship*. Valley Forge: Judson Press, 1983.

Chapter 5

The Educational Program

Church School or Sunday School

It really does not matter what a church chooses to call the organized teaching ministry structure. But "church school" seems to be used more frequently now than "Sunday school." Generations ago, Robert Raikes started "Sunday schools" for poor children in England which were schools in the broader sense—teaching some subjects other than the Bible and church matters. As the need for such schools became obsolete due to public education of all children, the Sunday school became part of the church program to teach the Bible and religion. So, most of the churches seem to prefer to call the organization the "church school" now and consider it on a par with all other parts of the total ministry. Now the church school is properly evaluated as an absolutely indispensable unit in the church program. It is the means of training people of all ages to live in the light of the Christian heritage, to come to terms with the necessity for personal commitment, and to grow in knowledge of the Bible and the church.

What Is Included in a Church School?

Generally, a church school is thought of as classes for as many age groups as the size of the church permits. These classes meet every Sunday morning, or as many Sunday mornings as the conditions of the church in its locality will determine; or the classes will meet at some other time on Sunday or during the week to meet whatever need there is to the best advantage.

And, in addition to classes, some church schools will plan for other allied activities, such as vacation church schools, weekday church schools in communities where this is desirable, Scouts, small discussion groups, and possibly other activities of a learning nature.

General Leadership

Before looking at the various activities of the church school let us take a brief look at the administrative leadership of the school.

1. *The Board of Christian Education.* Every church, no matter how large or small, needs to elect or appoint a group of people to take particular responsibility for the educational program. This group usually is called the board of Christian education. Because of the many involvements of this board, a separate report will be made in the next chapter.

2. *The Pastor.* In small churches, it is possible that the pastor will be the person with the widest knowledge and best training in the field of Christian education. In this event, he

or she will direct the program by advising and assisting the people selected by the church to bear the burdens of the school. Even in large churches the pastor is, to a large degree, the "teacher of teachers" due to his or her call and function in the church. In any event, the pastor should be an *ex officio* member of all the boards or committees in any way related to the educational program.

3. *The Volunteer Director of Education.* In churches with a budget that does not provide for a paid director of education, there may be found a person who works in the educational field outside the church, and who will utilize this professional knowledge and skill in the work of the church school. If such a person is willing to attend training conferences conducted by the denominational educational workers, an orientation to Christian education could be attained. Even in a church where there is no trained person available, one might be found to serve under the guidance of the pastor.

4. *The Paid Director of Christian Education.* A full-time director is to be desired if the church can make arrangements to engage such a person (assuming the church is large enough to warrant the addition of such a staff member). If funds are limited, a part-time director might be found at a nearby seminary or training school. The method of selecting a director and the major duties were covered in the first chapter, but an additional point worth mentioning is that the church should be informed as to the responsibilities and functions of this paid staff person. Unless there is a clear understanding, the director may be imposed upon by the membership and other staff by assuming that here is another member for the choir,

one who may be called upon to play the piano for some gathering, or who could fill in as secretary in an emergency. Also, without a clear understanding of the duties of this director, some lay leaders may repel or ignore suggestions or recommendations coming from that source.

The Sunday Church School

The term "Sunday church school" is used because the majority of our churches conduct the school on Sunday. It is understood that there are exceptions where circumstances favor another day of the week.

Undoubtedly, the traditional Sunday morning session of the church school plays the major role in Christian education. Here all ages are represented in an accepted organization planned with special emphasis on a systematic study of the Bible in order to understand its contents and how the teachings may be applied to life. Many of the pupils in this session of the school will be under the influence of its curriculum for many years. This is a choice opportunity for the growth of Christian character and the development of leadership. The lion's share of the appropriation for education may be invested profitably here, and the best leaders available should be challenged to give their time to this work.

1. *General Superintendent.*

(*a*) *The method of selection.* The superintendent is elected by the church, as a rule, although the board of Christian education should have the privilege of suggesting a name or names to the nominating committee. The tenure of office is one year with, usually, no limit on immediate and repeated reelection. Some churches, however, think it wise to put a limit on the total time of service—say five years.

(*b*) *Qualifications.* The chief requirements are administrative ability, leadership ability, tact, sound judgment, familiarity with up-to-date church school methods, a spirit of unselfish cooperation, and freedom to give much time to the job. Of course, to find all of these qualifications in one person is difficult, to say the least. In any event, the superintendent should be a person of genuine Christian commitment. The church school superintendent's influence can be of much value, particularly in a small community. In all communities it is likely that children and young people will observe this leader and be affected by what they see and hear.

(*c*) *Duties.* The tasks of the superintendent are as many and varied and exacting as the ideal qualifications.

(1) *Working under direction.* If the church school is to be an integral part of the total church program, the superintendent cannot do the work successfully independently of others working in the church. In a large church there will be a board of Christian education and a director to formulate plans and programs, which must be respected and followed. In a smaller church, the superintendent has recourse to the pastor as one having a more complete vision of the church objective. Thus, the superintendent is one of a team of loyal people working toward the goals set for the year.

(2) *Administration.* The superintendent is the chief executive of the Sunday morning session of the church school. Under the leadership of the superintendent will be a staff of volunteer workers (in rare instances there may be some paid

teachers) including, in a large school, an assistant superintendent, divisional superintendents for the various age groupings, a secretary, a librarian, a pianist, teachers, and substitute
teachers. In a small school there may be none to help except
the teachers. In any situation the superintendent will be responsible for defining the tasks of those who are workers and
for seeing that each one is busy at the job assigned. Equipment
that will be needed on Sunday morning must be made available by the superintendent in the places and at the time
required. Such equipment may include chalkboards, chalk
and erasers, Bibles, curriculum resources (papers, quarterlies,
and so forth), maps, pictures, visual aid apparatus, chairs, and
tables.

The superintendent should have a firm arrangement with
the teachers so that they will give ample warning of expected
absences in order that substitute teachers will be on hand. A
quick check of the school on Sunday morning may disclose
an unexpected teacher absence, which will call for immediate
action—a substitute may be secured or classes might be
combined. In addition to these obvious tasks of administration, all else that might be done to add to the efficiency of the
school will demand the attention of the superintendent. Some
of the administrative jobs may be taken over by staff members. For instance, each teacher might be made responsible
for checking needed equipment in ample time before the class
session, and someone might be willing to make the teacher
attendance check each week.

(3) *Presiding officer.* When there is occasion to have a
general assembly of the entire church school or an assembly

of certain age groups, the superintendent will preside. At business meetings of teachers and other staff, at special holiday events, and all other get-togethers the superintendent will preside. The superintendent will represent the Sunday church school at the meetings of the board of Christian education, the advisory (or executive) board, church meetings, and some community or interdenominational affairs. The superintendent is the "voice" of the morning session.

(4) *Ex officio adviser.* The superintendent is an ex officio member of all school committees and will be present or accounted for at all important meetings, keeping informed and adding to any discussion facts related to the total program. Most of the important planning work will be done in committees and in departmental or divisional groups; because of this the superintendent will be enabled to do administrative work in an unobtrusive and effectual way.

(5) *Spiritual leader.* The superintendent may well set a devotional pattern by including a brief period of Scripture reading and prayer to open staff meetings and assemblies. If feasible, a gathering of teachers and others before the opening session for a quiet moment and prayer could be most helpful. The superintendent will be on the alert to procure new books on the devotional life for the use of the workers. And the superintendent will make a habit of being at the morning church service!

(6) *Researcher.* The superintendent will do well to keep up on administrative skills by enrolling in courses available at leadership training schools in the area. If the superintendent is present for participation in these schools, the teachers and

others will place a greater value on what is being offered. In addition to courses, the superintendent may take time to read journals and books related to the work, visit sessions of other church schools, and evaluate every suggestion or program that is offered by the denomination. In the long run, a church school will be as progressive as the superintendent.

2. *Assistant Superintendent.* A person may be appointed (or elected) to work with the general superintendent and be the substitute when the superintendent must be absent. A small school may not need such a person, while a large school may need several assistants. Even in a small school, however, there may be some reasons for having this office. For instance: the present superintendent may have held office for years, may be aging, or may have announced a decision to relinquish the job at the end of the term. Under one or more of these conditions, it is wise to "break in" a person who could be eligible for the post on a permanent basis.

The assistant will be elected or appointed in the same manner as the superintendent, and the qualifications will be much the same, except that more latitude may be allowed on the side of experience. The chosen person will gain experience on the job.

The duties will depend largely on the personality of the superintendent. The assistant's job is to assist, and he or she will do those things delegated by the "chief." For one thing, the assistant usually makes the morning tour of the classes and departments to make sure that there are no unreported absences of workers. The superintendent may wish to give over to the assistant the task of ordering and procuring supplies.

And, of course, the assistant will take over in the superintendent's absence.

3. *Secretary.* Even in small schools a secretary is essential. Usually, the secretary is appointed by the superintendent, although sometimes the board of Christian education reserves the right of approval of the choice.

The primary task of the secretary is to keep the records. There will be a classbook, or set of attendance cards, for each class, which must be distributed before the class is in session and then collected as soon as the attendance has been marked. From these records, the secretary will make a summary of the number of officers, teachers, and pupils present, the amount of the offering (if the school takes class offerings), and any other details of interest to the school. This report will be given to the superintendent, who may wish to make some announcement of it at the close of the school, or the figures may be put on a wall record board.

The secretary's records are valuable, too, when graphs are made to show the trends in attendance and to compare with former years. Often a comparative graph will disclose weak spots in the school that merit special attention.

In addition to being the record-keeper, the secretary may take the minutes of workers' conferences and other business meetings of the school staff. A good secretary will make, or cause to be made, transcripts of the minutes for mailing to all staff members. Frequently, also, there will be letters to write, such as notifying members of their appointment to committees.

4. *Librarian.* In small schools, this office may be combined with that of secretary. The following duties may fall upon the

librarian. The librarian may make up the quarterly order for curriculum resources and other supplies in consultation with the superintendent or assistant. This order will cover lesson quarterlies, leaflets, workbooks, pictures, "story" papers, teachers' manuals, and many other items. After the arrival of the supplies, the librarian will be responsible for distributing them to the teachers and officers, and for keeping any surplus available for new enrollments or in the event of mislaid books. The efficiency with which this task is done will substantially affect the efficiency of the school. Teachers forced to improvise for even one Sunday without the aid of current materials may be handicapped for the entire quarter. And a new pupil who must wait for weeks for a book and other materials may quit in discouragement.

In schools maintaining a workers' library and/ or a library with books available to pupils, the librarian will be responsible for keeping the books in good condition, for keeping records of withdrawals and returns, for keeping a card catalog of the books available, and for ordering new books when authorized.

5. *Heads of divisions or departments*. In schools having several classes in each age group—children, youth, young adults, adults—there may be a need for a person at each age level to coordinate the work and have departmental meetings of teachers. These persons will make it a point to keep abreast of the developments in the age group represented—for instance, the head of the adult department will seek books and articles having to do with adult work in particular and will attend conferences devoted to that field.

Weekday Church School

The strong emphasis of former years on the weekday church school has gradually weakened until the prevalence of this activity is not widespread now. However, because this phase of church school work is of interest in some localities, a brief summary of its work and purpose is included in this report.

Inasmuch as weekday work is largely interdenominational and community-wide, a local church rarely has the privilege of naming the director. In community efforts, this official is elected at a meeting of representatives of all the churches involved. This group will include pastors, general superintendents, the chairperson of the board of Christian education from each church, directors of Christian education, associate pastors, and delegates-at-large (sometimes including representatives of the public schools involved). The meeting of this elective body comes in March or April, as a rule, and plans are made for the school year starting in September. The director, assistant director, secretary, and treasurer may be elected. Churches are assessed financially according to the number of their children to be enrolled; donations are invited from civic and church organizations. The money will be used for class materials, paid teachers (where adequately trained volunteers are not available), certificates of achievement, reimbursement of the expenses of the churches or other buildings used, and so forth.

The elected director and staff will plan the school in accordance with the laws, precedents, and needs of the community. The possibilities include:

(a) *Released-time classes.* In this setup, the classes leave the public school buildings and go to churches or other places provided by the staff. It is the responsibility of the director to furnish escorts to and from the public school building or buildings. At busy corners the local police may be utilized by arrangement with the town authorities, but the main job will be done by volunteers from the churches. The classes are permitted to be absent from public school for a set period, usually one class period or one hour.

Under released-time methods, the compulsion on the child to attend weekday school is dependent upon the parents. At the beginning of the school year, the public school teachers send home to the parents of the children a slip of paper which is to be signed to indicate if the child is or is not to be released for religious instruction, and in which group the child is to be included—Protestant, Catholic, or Jewish. With this slip goes a mimeographed sheet (supplied by the staff or the weekday school) describing the project.

When the hour arrives for the released time, four divisions are made of each class: one goes to the Protestant place of instruction, one to the Catholic, one to the Jewish, and the fourth continues with public school instruction (usually in a study-period arrangement). Under this released-time arrangement, the public school may demand that the teachers engaged by the weekday staff measure up to the same standards required of public school teachers. The course will be as closely integrated with the public school work as possible.

Weekday schools rarely start their work below the fourth

grade or continue it beyond the junior high level. This varies, of course, in each community.

The weekday school teachers grade their pupils as carefully as the public school teachers, and they are authorized to expect the same standard of discipline. The grades are passed on to the public school teachers for recording on the report cards. If the public school will not accept this responsibility, the weekday staff reports to the parents directly.

Commencement exercises are planned by the weekday staff, and certificates are awarded for completion of the work. Awards for excellence may be part of the program.

(b) *After school time.* In this arrangement, the public schools are not involved in granting absences from class, and no records will be kept of the pupils attending the class in religion. If the cooperation of the parents is of a high level and the program is inviting, a sufficient number of pupils may be found. Escorts meet the children at the public school at dismissal time and conduct them to the place of instruction.

(c) *Shared time.* This is a fairly new concept and may never gain wide acceptance. The philosophy of it is that no religious group should need to provide complete educational facilities on a separate basis; not only is there a financial burden, but also this separation prevents the daily mingling of all of the children in a community. In the shared time idea, all children would be in public schools except for those subjects that directly concern religious beliefs or sectarian ethical teaching. For these subjects, the various faiths would be responsible to take their children to church or synagogue at set times in the week and provide teachers and materials. If this plan materializes in any community, the churches will have more freedom to conduct the classes in a more positive way using a more specific curriculum.

Vacation Church School

The vacation church school is a summer session and may be from one to six weeks in length. The school may be conducted by one local church, by several churches of the same denomination, or by the community involving churches of several denominations (of late years, some communities have found it possible and good to bring Catholics into the project). Some advantages of any cooperative venture are that a staff may be gathered together more easily and the financing is less of a burden; also, with a larger group of children, closer grading is possible.

A vacation church school staff is appointed or elected in the manner of the weekday school staff if the work is community-wide. If a single church plans its own school, the staff will be gathered as for the Sunday morning session of the school. A general director or superintendent, an assistant, departmental supervisors, teachers, a secretary, a treasurer, a pianist, and specialists in certain activities (arts and crafts, for instance) will be needed.

Children will be invited to attend by means of publicity in the Sunday morning sessions of the church school, by posters placed in the church and in business establishments, by newspaper space and articles, and by mail invitations. An advance registration is essential in order that the size of the staff may be determined, space selected and allotted, and materials provided.

The curriculum of a school in a single church is easily arranged by those responsible in that church. A community school calls for many staff meetings to select the best from the offerings of the various agencies. In a community school, of course, sectarian bias is to be avoided.

The director will arrange financing according to the instructions given by the planners of the school. The entire sum may come from the church (or churches), or part may come from the church and part from gifts made in response to pleas for funds; some may come from registration fees and offerings taken in the school and at the commencement.

The sessions of a vacation church school extend, customarily, from nine in the morning until noon, Monday through Friday. The afternoons are free, except for picnics or other outings. The commencement and display of handwork may be an evening affair in order to get as many parents as possible. In some cases, the school is now being conducted in the early evening hours.

(Definite plans for the planning and conduct of a vacation church school are available from denominational sources and from interdenominational agencies.)

Summer Opportunities

In addition to the various phases of the church school discussed in this report, there are some summer possibilities.

Conferences, camps, retreats, day camps, picnics, hikes, directed playground work, nature study, and community service projects give a board of Christian education and other leaders openings for church school activities that may well contribute to the growth of Christian character and knowledge. Also, if the Sunday church school dwindles or is closed during the summer months, these extra things may hold the groups together for a vigorous start in the fall.

Helpful Books for Further Investigation

Blazier, Kenneth, and Isham, Linda, eds., *The Teaching Church at Work*, Revised Edition. Valley Forge: Judson Press, 1993.

Gehris, Paul D., and Gehris, Katherine A., *The Teaching Church—Active in Mission*. Valley Forge: Judson Press, 1987.

Huber, Evelyn, and Blazier, Kenneth, *Planning Christian Education in Your Church*. Valley Forge: Judson Press, 1974.

Chapter 6

The Board of Christian Education

Who Needs a Board of Christian Education?

Some have said that a church having 150 or fewer members does not need a board of Christian education. Others insist that the limited leadership available in a smaller church makes a board of Christian education a practical impossibility. Experience, however, points to the contrary, for in many churches of fewer than one hundred members there are effective boards of Christian education. Such boards usually operate with three elected members and two, or possibly three, *ex officio* members. The work is distributed among them, and, as in larger churches, others are drawn into the work of committees. The board will do many things while sitting as a committee-of-the-whole.

The Board of Christian Education

The board of Christian education is a group of persons selected by a church for the purpose of unifying all of the

Christian education organizations, activities, and efforts of the local church, to create and promote essential activities hitherto omitted, and to coordinate all similar or duplicate efforts.

1. *How organized*. A church without a board of Christian education, and with no provision for one in the church constitution, will need to prepare and submit for adoption a bylaw that details the organization and responsibilities of the board.

2. *How Elected*. The bylaw will provide for election procedures, but the most efficient method has proved to be that of electing one-third of the board annually. The regular nominating committee will bring in these names with others on the slate. A board of three persons will be rotated so that one member is elected each year; a board of six will need two new members each year, etc. If the members of the board are made ineligible for reelection until after the lapse of a year, a rotating board will become the natural result.

3. *The Membership*. The pastor of the church, the director of Christian education (paid or voluntary), and the general superintendent of the church school should be *ex officio* members of the board. All other members will be elected by the church. The board should be made up of a sufficient number of persons to give adequate attention to all that is included in the church's total educational program, including work with children, youth, and adults.

The size of the board depends largely on local conditions and will be determined primarily by the size of the church. A church of one hundred or fewer members should have a board of three, a church of two to four hundred needs six, and a church of five hundred or over may require nine. By including *ex officio* committee members from outside the personnel of the board, the largest church need not go over nine elected members. The elected members are not to be selected on the basis of their activity in some educational organization of the church, such as Sunday church school youth organization, or Scouts, inasmuch as this would reduce the board to a council of related activities. Nor should the board be too heavily loaded with people whose chief efforts have been in the Sunday church school. Perhaps the following statement of qualifications will help explain all of this.

4. *Qualifications of Members.* Christian character is the first consideration among the qualifications, just as is true of deacons, trustees, and others, and is essential in this work, which directly affects the Christian growth of members of the church and their children. The nominating committee is justified in looking for the evidence of personal religious experience as shown by activity as a church member.

It is possible, however, for a person to be admirable in experience and activity and yet limit that activity to one particular project. Such a person should be left to that favorite project, for the board needs people of broad interests in the many-sided program of the church.

Even granted these two qualifications, we have not yet described the "ideal" board member. An ideal member will have the two basic qualifications: an open mind and an eagerness to learn with a capacity for growth. In no other field are methods and resources changing so rapidly as in the field of education. The board member needs to be one who is willing to investigate new materials and new approaches. The person should be familiar with approved methods in education and, if possible, should have some experience in education.

Of course, the average church will not be able to find enough "ideal" members available for even a small board. The nominating committee must approximate the ideal and counter the weakness of one member with the strength of another so that the board will have always represented (1) deep, personal religious experience, (2) wide interests, (3) possibilities for mental and spiritual growth, and, if possible, (4) experience in the best educational procedures.

5. *Organization.* Unless the church has designated the officers of the board, an organizational meeting should be held soon after the church election to select the chairperson and secretary. At this meeting, preliminary work can be done on setting up committees and assigning responsibility to members of the board. Where the board is large enough for specialized work, the organization should provide for chairpersons of children's work, youth work, adult work, leadership education, and missions and stewardship education. Each of these chairpersons will have a working committee of those involved in the respective activity. It cannot be stressed too strongly that the board must operate functionally. Because there is frequently misunderstanding concerning the relationship of *ex officio* members, it may be well to look at some guiding principles. First, let it be clear that an *ex officio* member is one who is a member of the board by virtue of the other office that is held. Such a member has full privileges, including the right to vote on all matters coming before the

board, and should be used on subcommittees. However, an *ex officio* member is not counted when determining a quorum.

6. *Duties*. The tasks of the board crisscross and intertwine, but for the sake of classification they may be looked at under five general heads: administration, leadership, curriculum, outreach, and program.

(*a*) Administration will include an annual survey of the total educational program of the church with an evaluation as to worth of each activity, adoption of standards and goals of the work, the allotting of space in the building to the activities, and the preparation of a budget.

(*b*) Leadership will be concerned with searching for leaders, selecting leaders, training leaders, and encouraging leaders.

(*c*) Curriculum will involve consultation with workers as to the selection and use of resource materials. The aim will be to utilize the best available material that can be used by the teaching staff and to make sure that there is a unity of use so that there is no gap in the overall learning experience of the pupils made by the introduction of materials at variance with the selected resources.

(*d*) Outreach is a self-explanatory word. The work of Christian education will not be confined to the presently enrolled members of the various activities but will be extended by reaching out to the hitherto unreached, to church families and homes, and into the community.

(*e*) An adequate program of Christian education in the local church will include all possible areas, such as the Sunday church school, vacation church school, weekday church school (where this is a possibility), youth organizations, mission, leadership and stewardship education, student counseling, camping, and family life programs. Specific information about each of these areas is available from denominational offices and interdenominational agencies.

It is important to repeat that all members of the board of Christian education need to be familiar with the total educational work of their church.

Helpful Books for Further Investigation

Blazier, Kenneth D., and Isham, Linda, eds., *The Teaching Church at Work*, Revised Edition. Valley Forge: Judson Press, 1993.

Cober, Kenneth, *Shaping the Church's Educational Ministry*. Valley Forge: Judson Press, 1971.

Heusser, D-B and Phyllis, *Children as Partners in the Church*. Valley Forge: Judson Press, 1985.

Ng, David, *Youth in the Community of Disciples*. Valley Forge: Judson Press. 1984.

Chapter 7

In Conclusion

The following conclusions may be drawn from this study:

1. Our church is a lively part of the great Christian enterprise.

2. This enterprise has its roots in the New Testament.

3. A church cannot operate successfully without officers and teachers.

4. Every officer has a specific function or group of functions not included in the job description of any other official.

5. The work and responsibility of each officer is well documented in the records of the Christian church, and our reports have been based on reliable resources.

6. The nominating committee is a vital link between the church membership and the potential leadership being sought.

Appendix A

Organizing a Church

Let us think of a Baptist family moving into a new community. On Sunday morning this family looks about for a church nearby and finds none. As the days go on, the father and mother meet other men and women who are looking for a church for themselves and their children and for a Sunday church school. Someone suggests getting together to discuss the matter of a church, but not all are Baptists. Should they start several competitive and struggling groups or seek a way to worship together without asking anyone to give up denominational convictions?

A call to the nearest Baptist regional office will bring help. In fact, it is quite possible that that office has been working with representatives of other denominations to discover how the new housing area can be best served.

It may be that through cooperation between the people in the housing area and the Baptist office a plan for a community Baptist church may be arranged, each family thus receiving the best leadership possible because all agree to share in an adequate ministry. Under other circumstances, it may be that a group of Baptists is large enough to initiate plans for a Baptist church. Every group will have to determine which plan is best for the community—a denominational church or a denominationally sponsored community church. In due time, under either plan, a meeting is called, a group gathers, a moderator is selected, and business may be transacted. As soon as the moderator is elected, that person will take charge and call for the election of a clerk or secretary.

The gathered group will then elect or appoint a committee to draw up a tentative constitution. A date will be set for the next meeting at which this committee is to report. The adjournment of the first meeting will be by common consent.

The committee on the constitution will now start work. Probably those on the committee will secure copies of the constitutions of their former home churches. Copies of model constitutions may be had from denominational offices. Using these samples as guides only, the committee will prepare a constitution that it thinks is adapted to the needs of the new church in the new community. Committee members will realize that their work will be changed by revisions that will come out of the next meeting of the church-to-be. This is a reality that every constitutional committee must recognize, since it is a rare occurrence for such a committee to be appointed with "power."

At the next meeting, after the moderator has declared that the report of the committee is in order, a free and frank discussion will be held. In all likelihood, some, if not all, of the articles in the constitution will be changed; also, additional articles may be inserted. The constitution will set forth the purpose of the organization, the name of the church, the officers and committees to be elected, with their duties and responsibilities and powers, an article of rules concerning membership, the time and place of meetings, and the financial resources and program. After the adoption of the constitution and the election of the officers named in it, the group is essentially a church. In some states the church will not be recognized legally until the clerk has filed a copy of the constitution with the secretary of state, together with a petition for a charter to be granted by the state legislature. Customarily (although state regulations vary), if the constitution and the filing are in order, a charter will be granted at the next regular meeting of the legislature.

Locally and legally, the congregation is now a church. The church will decide upon its affiliations (see Appendix B) and apply for membership in the selected larger fellowships. A service of recognition of the church, with representatives of the denomination and other groups in the community present, should be arranged as soon as possible.

There remains only the calling of a pastor, and the church will be ready to function autonomously in the congregational tradition. The church will remain in existence until the members vote it out of existence or until it fails to live up to the constitution on which it is based.

Appendix B

A Church's Wider Relationships

The organization of one church is essentially the same as that of every other Baptist church in the world. Organization, association, administration, and activities are what are termed autonomous—determined by the members without outside authority. This being true, the church may choose its wider relationships. The groups to be considered for affiliation are:

1. *The Association or Cluster.* Fellowship and cooperation with other Baptist churches are privileges of a church. Such relationships are established and maintained by voluntary action of the membership.

If the decision is to be part of the nearest Association or Cluster (of Associations), the pastor and a certain number of members (as determined by the provisions of the larger body) will be elected by the church as delegates. The delegates will attend the Association (or Cluster) meetings and bring reports back to the church. The church will be requested to file with the clerk of the Association statistics showing accessions, losses, membership in numbers, financial status, church school information, and any other facts that will be of interest and value in the annual report. The expenses of the Association—cost of reports and other incidentals, the honoraria for special speakers, and so forth—are paid from the income received as dues from the member churches.

Associations (Clusters) have no power over Baptist churches. They are the churches in action on a regional scale. Some Associations conduct local mission enterprises and speak out on social issues. Also, training schools for participation in national denominational programs may be arranged by the Association.

The former importance of the Association as a powerful link between neighboring churches has decreased as transportation and communication have improved. Today, a state-wide gathering of churches raises no greater difficulties than an associational meeting did in years gone by. However, there are still distinct values in this fellowship of adjacent churches, inspiration and information being two of the most important.

A member church of an Association is considered to be a member of the state organization unless the church takes action otherwise.

2. *The American Baptist Churches of the State or Region* (formerly known as State Convention, and this designation still holds true in some areas). This grouping is the combining of the churches in a state or region for voluntary cooperation in enterprises too extended to be cared for by local churches alone or in associations. This work may include some mission work, the collecting of funds for special causes, cooperation

with the national organization in promoting the World Mission Budget (the unified budget of the American Baptist Churches in the U.S.A.).

The American Baptist Churches in a state maintain a staff to service the member churches. These staff persons may be in the fields of world mission support, evangelism, continuing education for pastors, Christian education, camping, etc. The trend is for staff members to be responsible for area supervision—that is, the person who has continuing education may also live within a designated area of the state or region as the "in-residence" representative of the state organization. The churches within that area look to that person to serve them and secure for them special help in any field of church life. The general executive of the state organization is known as the Executive Minister who administers the total program. The expenses of this state setup are met by a national return of a certain proportion of the mission money contributed by the churches within that state or region. The state organization has much to offer the local church by way of trained leadership in many fields and by helping in the locating of pastors for pastorless churches; financing of new buildings may be arranged by the executive minister. Inasmuch as each state or region has its own philosophy of service, the local church would be wise to become well acquainted with its own state organization.

3. *The City Society*. Since the reorganization of the regions of the American Baptist Churches, some City Societies have been merged with the state organizations or regional groupings, but there remain some large cities with their own local

organization, which functions much as the state group. A church that is a member of a City Society is, at least nominally, an integral part of the state organization as well. The name now used by most City Societies is (for example): The American Baptist Churches of metropolitan New York. In Philadelphia the Philadelphia Baptist Association is a historic title; it is the oldest Baptist grouping in the United States.

4. *The American Baptist Churches.* The church has one more link that relates it directly to the whole world mission of Baptists. The American Baptist Churches in the U.S.A. is successor to a long line of agencies organized to carry forward mission activities. After the separation of the southern and northern churches, the name used was Northern Baptist Convention. In 1950 the name was changed to American Baptist Convention. In 1972 the present name—American Baptist Churches in the U.S.A.—was adopted. There are a number of other national Baptist bodies, the largest of which is the Southern Baptist Convention.

In the American Baptist Churches the voluntary relationship is very strong. The raising of the great World Mission budget every year is the responsibility of the Churches' Division of World Mission Support, but it is the hearty participation of each church that brings the goal in sight.

The program boards of the American Baptist Churches are made up of persons who come from Baptist churches, and each board reports to the churches at the national convention. An annual printed report is also provided to the churches.

All of this activity in the association (cluster), state, and national groups is the work of local churches in free cooperation.

5. *The Baptist World Alliance.* This is a fellowship of Baptists the world around. Study groups and commissions pool the knowledge and experience of Baptists in the various countries, and there is an annual gathering for information and report.

6. *Councils of Churches.* There are local, state, national, and world councils of churches that a local church may consider as possibilities for affiliation. The church will study the program and goals of a council to learn whether or not the church is in sympathy with what is being done. The advantage of a council is that the local church has the opportunity to cooperate with churches of other denominations. There is no automatic membership from one council to another, and a church may belong to its community council without having any union with a state or world council, and vice versa.

7. Each community has its own groups that are organized to advance the cooperative work of the churches. After a church is well established, it may make a survey of what is available and decide to what extent it desires to work with other bodies.

Index